Guitar *signature licks*®

Audio Access Included

Roy Bucha[nan]

A Step-by-Step Breakdown of His Guitar Styles and Techniques

by Dave Rubin

To access audio visit:
www.halleonard.com/mylibrary

Enter Code
2145-8813-6626-3652

Guitar performed by L.J. Paten

Cover photo by Frans Schellekens/Redferns © Getty

ISBN 978-1-4584-9735-2

HAL•LEONARD®
CORPORATION
7777 W. BLUEMOUND RD. P.O. BOX 13819 MILWAUKEE, WI 53213

Visit Hal Leonard Online at
www.halleonard.com

DEDICATION AND ACKNOWLEDGMENTS

I want to dedicate this book to all those who want to make their guitar cry and have been touched by the music of Roy Buchanan. I am greatly indebted to renowned writer Phil Carson, the author of *Roy Buchanan: American Axe*, for the wealth of information in his definitive biography, his encouragement, and the rare, early recordings he graciously sent.

CONTENTS

PAGE TITLE

ROY BUCHANAN:
WHEN A GUITAR PLAYS THE BLUES

There are guitar heroes who achieve prominence through the development of astounding technique in the service of extraordinary musical expression. Then there are those few exceptions, like Jimi Hendrix, whose power to move us goes beyond that of mere mortals and seems to come from some otherworldly place. Roy Buchanan occupies a niche in that exclusive pantheon. A troubled, tortured spirit with mind-bending chops and the soul of a deep bluesman who could wave his hands over an inert plank of ash to make it come alive like the Sorcerer's Apprentice, he left behind an expansive legacy of blues, country, rockabilly, and rock music.

FROM THE OZARKS TO BAKERSFIELD

Roy once claimed he was "half wolf," but the facts reveal Leroy Buchanan was born to sharecroppers Bill and Minnie in Ozark, Arkansas, on September 23, 1939. In 1941, the family relocated to Pixley, California, near Bakersfield, in the San Joaquin Valley, where they labored in the fields, chasing the crops in a manner similar to migrant workers. When Leroy was 5, he heard his 16-year-old big brother, J.D., and friends playing guitars and, upon informing them that they were out of tune, preceded to correct the pitch in response to their challenge. Shortly thereafter, his father bought him a cheap, toy acoustic, but after it was broken by a cousin, it would be years before he would play again.

Following WWII, the Buchanans moved back to the Ozarks, only to return again to Pixley by way of iconic Route 66. Wanting more for her children than just a life of hardscrabble toil, in 1948, Minnie arranged for music lessons for Leroy from Mrs. Clara Louese Presher. A red Rickenbacker lap steel was purchased in part with funds sent from J.D., who was in the Army at the time. Leroy would have preferred a flat top acoustic, but his parents felt that he would have a better chance to stand out on the steel guitar, with so few players in the area. Unknown at the time was how the melancholy that pervaded the Buchanan family would combine with his basically taciturn nature to affect the emotional content of his music and life.

Listening to the Grand Ole Opry and other country music stations on the radio exposed Buchanan to a variety of songs that he would learn quickly by ear. "Step It Up and Go," by the Maddox Brothers and Rose (with the hot, young picker Roy Nichols), would exert a strong influence, along with black gospel music and eventually the blues. After three years, Mrs. Presher was dismayed to the point of tears that her talented student learned by ear instead of reading music, as she insisted. The fingerpicking skills he acquired on the steel, along with the sound, however, would serve him well later on when his amazingly fluid bending and sustain would come to characterize his personal style. Even more significant was his teacher's admonishment to always play with *feeling*, which was like telling a rooster to crow for day.

As a shy 12 year-old, Buchanan made his first public appearances playing recitals in his mother's church and at school assemblies, where he would amaze his friends by perfectly reproducing the steel-guitar parts and tone from Hank Williams' songs. He was invited to play steel with much older musicians in the Waw Keen Valley C&W band, and he became the "star" even though, as a minor, he had to sit behind a partition at establishments that served alcohol. Nonetheless, playing a six-string acoustic still intrigued him, and in 1952, at the age of 14, he acquired an f-hole Harmony and then a flat top Martin with a pickup in the sound hole in order to try to emulate Roy Nichols, who was then Merle Haggard's lead guitarist. Buchanan would get to see both Nichols and Buck Owens in person as they helped pioneer the raunchy, honky-tonk Bakersfield sound in the 1950s that fired his desire even more. In the meantime, he continued playing the steel in public.

FROM COUNTRY TO ROCK 'N' ROLL AND THE BLUES

A pivotal moment occurred in 1955, when Buchanan heard the Elvis Presley version of Little Junior Parker's "Mystery Train" on the radio. He would become enamored with the lead guitarist, Scotty Moore, going on to learn all his solos note-for-note. His fortuitous, if not preordained, exposure to the blues would happen in the black clubs in Stockton, California, on jaunts accompanying J.D. while big brother was on leave from the Army. It would critically change his outlook on music and the guitar, as he became determined to learn how to bend strings like the bluesmen. Around the same time, he also "discovered" jazz through guitarist Barney Kessel and his *Vol. 3: To Swing or Not to Swing* from 1955 and commenced to learning "modern" chords on the six-string. In addition, Roy Nichols would become an ever larger influence, even directly affecting the way Buchanan would develop his patented "backwards" phrasing in his soloing.

He formed the Dusty Valley Boys in high school to play the honky-tonk music that blended blues and C&W and was evolving in Bakersfield. Performing first at school assemblies, Buchanan still leaned on the steel for some tunes and even went so far as to fashion a homemade set up to imitate the new pedal steel that was just being introduced into country music. The band was expanded to include some older cats so they could get real paying jobs in liquor establishments, and they procured a steady gig at the nearby Forty-Niner club. In a phenomenon that would occur later in his career, people were soon lining up to see the band featuring Buchanan on an early 1950s hollowbody Gibson L-5. Included in their sets was the early rock 'n' roll of Bill Haley and Fats Domino, which Buchanan would always love and draw on for inspiration.

L.A. AND THE HEARTBEATS

Restless, depressed with living in rural Pixley, and driven by his ambition, he headed to Stockton to try to play full time, only to return broke and hungry. A chance trip to Hollywood with J.D. and some friends would show him the next step forward, however. With his brother settling in Los Angeles and his married older sister living nearby, Buchanan quit school and moved to Southern California to join his siblings. An aversion to the kind of manual labor J.D. and his brother-in-law envisioned for him led to getting hooked up with a shady, two-bit Hollywood hustler. Recognizing the guitarist's talent and naiveté and providing him a room in his apartment, the "promoter" built a band around him and future Jefferson Airplane drummer Spencer Dryden in 1956 called the Heartbeats, replete with cheesy, matching striped jackets. They played mostly simple, blues-based instrumentals that Dryden would "compose" after listening to R&B radio for ideas. The "highlight" of the Heartbeats' approximately six-month association would seem to be their brief appearance lip-syncing in a teen exploitation film called *Rock, Pretty Baby*.

Around this time, Buchanan made some home recordings with the help of his brother-in-law that featured solo country blues, "Nine-Pound Hammer," and a country instrumental that, while competent, barely suggests where he would soon be going. Concurrently, he was listening to the jazz of Tal Farlow, as well as Kessel, along with the blues guitar of Jimmy Nolen, then playing in the Johnny Otis band. Nolen, who is universally credited with helping invent funk guitar in the mid 1960s with James Brown, was an aggressive guitarist whose style, attitude, and version of the classic slow blues "After Hours" would have a huge influence on Buchanan, as did the blues of Blind Boy Fuller and Pete Lewis. Still trying to jump start his career, in 1957, he went back out on the road with a new lineup of the Heartbeats, minus Dryden and over the objections of his brother-in-law. His reward would be to end up stranded in Oklahoma City. Instead of returning to L.A., however, Buchanan returned to his family in Arkansas, where he would remain for a spell, in the bosom of his kin.

DALE HAWKINS

On the way back out west in 1958, Buchanan caught a break by landing a staff guitar position at a TV station in Tulsa. Fortuitously, it would lead to him backing Louisiana's Dale Hawkins, who came through town while touring the country on the back of his classic hit "Susie-Q." Released the previous year on Chess Records, it featured a young James Burton playing the signature riff. After hearing the raw 19 year-old, the "Shreveport Tornado" invited him to Louisiana for what would be two whirlwind years on the road playing hard-edged R&B and rock 'n' roll almost nightly. The experience would teach Buchanan how to pop strings and pills. The former involved the development of virtuoso chops that would allow him and just a drummer to accompany Hawkins with extraordinary expertise on occasion. He would also make his first official recordings, including the instrumental "Crossties," the B side of "La-Do-Dada," which hit #32 on the Billboard Top 40 charts for Hawkins, and "Lulu." He alternated gigs in brother Jerry Hawkins' band while Burton was still holding down the guitar chair with Dale, and the two future guitar heroes would find time together to jam and become friends and "friendly rivals." Later, both would claim to having pioneered the use of light banjo strings to facilitate bluesy string bending. Dale Hawkins would also shepherd his charges to Chess Studios in Chicago, where, among other tracks, they waxed a version of "My Babe," which showcased Buchanan's "dead thumb" technique and rockabilly solo on his L-5, along with other tracks on which he is not heard. Visits to the steamy Southside blues clubs, where the band hung out with Muddy Waters, Howlin' Wolf, Little Walter, and Willie Dixon, would make an impression with regard to illicit recreational lifestyle choices.

In 1959, Buchanan left Hawkins concurrently with the rockabilly cat's star fading due to a lack of radio hits. He went back to Louisiana to play with Jerry Hawkins and his estimable guitarist, Joe Osborn. Scuffling for work, they took a road trip to L.A. with their song "Linda Lu." In a perhaps apocryphal story, they were paid $30 by Ebb Records for the recording, along with the promise that it would be released. Instead, the tune was given to bluesman Ray Sharpe, who copied their arrangement in total and subsequently had a major R&B hit with it in 1959 on the Jamie label.

The L.A. lifestyle did not appeal to Hawkins, and he left quickly. Buchanan and Osborn hooked up with country singer Bob Luman, who had just lost James Burton to budding teen idol and TV star Ricky Nelson, and they accompanied him to Las Vegas in his troupe. Osborn recalled that it was during this time that Buchanan traded his L-5 for his first Telecaster, having been intrigued with the instrument ever since seeing Buck Owens and Roy Nichols play them, though there is disagreement as to when this "mythological moment" may actually have occurred. Recording with the Elvis-envying Luman on "Buttercup," and particularly on the primeval and raucous instrumental "Roy's Guitar Boogie," hints at the genesis of his wildly eclectic style. After a landmark tour of Japan, the gig with Luman ended, and Buchanan and Osborn settled back in glamorous Las Vegas and scuffled until Dale Hawkins came calling again in 1960. "Rescuing" the two guitarists, he sent them to New Jersey to back his brother Jerry in a lounge show. When that engagement ended, they once again returned to Louisiana, where James Burton would snare Osborn to play bass behind Ricky Nelson in Hollywood in an event that would eventually lead to the guitarist becoming a top studio four-stringer with the "Wrecking Crew" in L.A. However, being based in Shreveport afforded continual recording opportunities for Buchanan, including on "Loretta" with singer Al Jones and "So Lonely" behind Bobby Jay, though they brought neither fame nor fortune.

Meanwhile, Hawkins swooped back in yet another time to take Buchanan out on the road. The years 1960–61 found the singer and his lead guitarist recording tracks produced by Leiber and Stoller in New York City, in addition to Buchanan appearing with Hawkins on his Philadelphia rock 'n' roll TV show. On the road in Washington, D.C., Buchanan was asked to play on a session behind the Perry Mates in exchange for being allowed to record his first instrumental version of "After Hours." Fully in evidence is his virtuosic string manipulation and ear for melodies that would eventually propel him to legendary underground status among guitarists and fans. He was only 21 years old at the time.

With proper promotion by the Bomarc label, a Swan subsidiary, the record may have gone somewhere in an era when instrumentals were common and popular on the radio. Instead, Buchanan was compelled to keep touring behind Hawkins, including two trips to Canada. On the second jaunt, they ran into cousin Ronnie Hawkins and his band, the Hawks, in Toronto. Recognizing his consummate skills in backing a singer, Ronnie stole Buchanan away from Dale so he could tutor his young, up-and-coming guitarist, Robbie Robertson. The pedagogy lasted a month and would have a far reaching effect on Robertson, as well as impressing the Hawks drummer, the late Levon Helm. When Dale Hawkins decided to go his own way, Buchanan returned to Washington, where he formed the Saxtons with the tenor saxist and drummer from the Hawkins touring band. They would evolve into the Bad Boys and played stomping roadhouse rock 'n' roll to enthusiastic crowds in the D.C.-Maryland-Virginia area.

FROM FAMILY LIFE IN MARYLAND TO BACK ON THE ROAD AGAIN

In the summer of 1961, Buchanan married Judy Owens, a "fan" who had been after him, on and off, for years. However, sedate family life did not set well with him after the "high" life on the road (and the requisite number of amphetamines that it entailed), and he jumped at the chance, with Judy in tow, to record with Ronnie Hawkins and the Hawks in New York City, even if it meant humbling himself by playing bass behind Robertson. A "stinging" version of "Farther on Up the Road" with Helm on vocals and drums proved that the junior axe man had learned his lessons well. As would happen continually throughout his badly mismanaged career, Buchanan ended up with little or nothing to show for his efforts.

Broke and hungry once again, on the way back, they stopped off in the Philadelphia area, where Buchanan was graciously hooked up with the rocking 'n' rolling Bobby Moore and the Temptations (later the Temps) by a DJ acquaintance. Settling temporarily in South Jersey with Judy, he would stay with the Temps until early 1963. Besides slowly building a reputation from roadhouse to roadhouse as a brilliant guitarist, he was given the chance to record on Dick Clark's Swan Records in late 1961. Included were "Ruby, Baby;" "Mule Train Stomp;" "Pretty Please;" and, under the pseudonym "the Secrets," "Hot Toddy" and "Twin Exhaust." In 1963, "Mary Lou," "The Shuffle," "Braggin'," and "Trophy Run" were added to his Temps output. All showed an aspect of his growing confidence and eclectic ability. Recording with Moore led to sessions for other Swan artists, including Freddie "Boom Boom" Cannon and Danny & the Juniors, whose "Twist Medley" contains an African-American vulgarity slipped into the vocal chorus, much like the All-Stars would do behind Junior Walker on "Shotgun" in 1965.

THE PINCH HARMONIC

Bobby Gregg, a session drummer for Swan Records who would go on to back an impressive list of notable artists, convinced Buchanan to record a hip riff that he was playing in the studio as "The Jam (Pts. 1 & 2)" under the name Bobby Gregg & His Friends. The instrumental reached #14 on the R&B charts in 1962 and became a must-know for aspiring guitar heroes, even though Gregg stole the publishing credit while teaching Buchanan a hard lesson that he would never forget. Historically, however, it is the groovy instrumental "Potato Peeler" with Gregg that is most remembered. At 0:53 in the track, Buchanan plays an accidental "pinch harmonic" in his opening solo for what is considered to be the first time on record. He was quoted as saying that he was trying to reproduce the squealing sound that honking R&B tenor sax players routinely used for musical punctuation, and it would become one of his trademarks, as well as an accepted part of the language of rock guitar.

By the time his tenure with the Temps ended in conflict, Buchanan was well on his way to becoming an underground legend in the Mid-Atlantic states. None other than Les Paul had heard of his prowess and tracked him down in New Jersey, helping to spread the word about a guy who plays "like no one else." However, due to a variety of factors, including his baffling personality, unpredictable behavior, and the birth of his second child, he, Judy, and their children moved into Judy's mother's home in suburban Maryland in the spring of 1963. The metropolitan Washington, D.C., area offered numerous opportunities to play country, rock 'n' roll, and R&B music in the many clubs, often catering to servicemen, that dotted the region, and there were the requisite number of great musicians to provide it. In what must have been a crushing blow to his sense of pride, Buchanan was reportedly compelled to sell encyclopedias before finding work with the sax-led Saxtons and lounge singer Danny Denver and the Soundtracks. A more substantial gig, however, was scored in 1964 with singer/guitarist Bobby Howard, who had recently backed Link Wray. Performing as the Hi-Boys, they would respond to the rampant popularity of the British Invasion by renaming their band the British Walkers and adopting matching suits and "Beatles" haircuts. Their single "I Found You" from the same year is a reasonable, if cynical, facsimile of the "Mersey Beat" sound from across the Atlantic, with two short, melodic Buchanan guitar solos. When Howard found it necessary to go out on the road without Buchanan in 1965, the erstwhile sideman went scuffling again. He appears at that point to have lost the driving ambition of his earlier career, becoming resigned and bitter about the pursuit of fame. Still, as would happen every so often, his immense talent and growing legend was recognized by a local big band drummer who invited him to teach guitar in his shop in order to get by. He only lasted three months before quitting by simply not showing up one day for his students.

Through the rest of the 1960s, Buchanan operated out of the D.C. area as an over qualified sideman while continuing to attract the attention of humbled guitarists and ecstatic fans. A string of local bands, including the Outcasts and the Kalin Twins, who had a hit in 1958 with "When," only served to bolster his status with every appearance, as he was being advertised as "Mr. Guitar Himself." On one particular occasion, he sat in at a black club and "cut the head" of Bobby Parker, the reigning D.C. guitar hero, to the utter dismay of the "brother." In the fall of 1966, he packed up Judy, who felt the need to keep an eye on her husband, and their family for a stint at the Jersey shore with the Monkey Men, a wildly theatrical rock group that actually further encouraged Buchanan to indulge his creativity and seemingly boundless imagination to the delight of all.

Back home in suburban Maryland in the fall of 1967, he found plenty of work in the hip Georgetown section of D.C., particularly at the Silver Dollar, where he felt free to occasionally indulge his staggering skills, while still plodding along in bands not worth his talent, including the Devil's Sons, the Outsiders, the Four Skins, and the Fourmost, who were sometimes called Uncalled Four. While playing with the Poor Boys, he returned to the Jersey shore as a home base from which to gig in the Philly and surrounding Pennsylvania area through 1967. As he was then known to do on the bandstand, Buchanan would blow the doors off the joint with his solo, virtuosic version of "Malaguena." Unfortunately, a previous night of heavy drinking in Wildwood, New Jersey, with his old mates from the Tempts resulted in him going way overboard by playing like a mad man on the bar and at his gig the next night. Later, he tried to attack a member of the Poor Boys back at their apartment complex. As a result, everyone connected with the band had to flee, including Judy and their children.

HENDRIX

The year 1968 would prove to be a pivotal one for Buchanan. Although a planned meeting unfortunately never occurred, seeing Hendrix in person on the shooting star's second trip through D.C. would command his admiration and give him new material to work into his repertoire. Simultaneously, it also had a depressing influence, as he realized that the virtuosic techniques that he had developed with a Telecaster, the small Fender Vibrolux, and just his hands, such as long, sinuous sustain, distortion, feedback, wah-wah effects, and volume swells, were now available to anyone through stomp boxes and stacks of high powered amps. Also evident was the outrageous showmanship that audiences now craved, but that Buchanan would never be comfortable with attempting, though he could easily reproduce the licks of Hendrix, Clapton, and the other famous rock guitarists of the era. Instead, he resolved to stay with what he did best, which was to reach deeper into his soul than most and express his profound feelings on the blues, country, and rock 'n' roll with his enormous skills. But the local, low paying gigs were grinding him and his wife, so when the successful country/pop lounge lizard Danny Denver came calling again to join the Soundmasters, he acceded, though it was no improvement to his situation, even with the recording of *Live! At the Stardust*. A short stay in Nashville with the help of friends was disastrous, as his long time substance abuse that consisted of amphetamines washed down with beer was catching up with him.

When he returned to Maryland, he enrolled in barber school, an ironic decision considering his always challenging hairstyles. Leaving the pressures of the music business for a regular middle class lifestyle now seemed appealing and appeared to be a relief as Judy bore their fifth child. He graduated in August 1969, just before Woodstock, as the counterculture era was unfortunately passing by one of the greatest guitarists of all time. One significant highlight from this low point, however, occurred when Buchanan traded his Les Paul for his iconic 1953 Telecaster. Though there would be another demoralizing misstep coming his way, the breakthrough that he so richly deserved was only slightly "further on down the road."

CHARLIE DANIELS AND THE CROSSROADS

Tiring of barbering, Buchanan started thinking about that old Tele in the case and perhaps slipping back in again with Danny Denver, who once bragged that he would be bigger than Elvis. Coinciding with his itch to get out and play again, his old acquaintance Charlie Daniels showed up with a contract and a modest advance from Polydor Records to cut an album in Nashville. Several sessions over a period of months through early 1970 produced the misguided *The Prophet*. With the results disappointing to all concerned, it thankfully remained unreleased until 2004, except for a few select tracks that appear on *Sweet Dreams: The Anthology*. Daniel's original "Black Autumn" does contain two instrumental sections with the chord changes and dramatic melody of what would later become Buchanan's "The Messiah Will Come Again," but his unique skills and creativity were mostly thwarted and the experience only contributed to his discouragement.

Nonetheless, he went back to playing with the delusional Denver, who had a steady gig with his Soundmasters at a redneck roadhouse in suburban Maryland called the Crossroads Restaurant and Supper Club. It would be a mighty stretch to compare it to Robert Johnson going to the mythical "crossroads" in the Delta for immortality, but the funky gin mill would figure prominently in the lore of his "discovery" and eventual rise from obscurity. For five sets, six nights a week, in 1970, Buchanan chafed under the tight restraint that Denver applied to his creativity as people showed up to see the amazing sideman cut loose rather than hear the lead singer croon the current pop and country hits of the day. Meanwhile, hippies and hipsters were making the pilgrimage to the Crossroads to catch the incendiary guitarist who stood stock still while drawing forth previously unimagined sounds from his battered Tele. The mix of conservative and liberal lifestyles would sometimes make for a volatile atmosphere, even as throngs of musicians started coming to hear what the underground buzz was all about. A laudatory story in the *Washington Post* about Buchanan by rock journalist and amateur drummer Tom Zito was followed by it being reprinted in *Rolling Stone* in early 1971, and contemporary guitar stars like Eric Clapton, Peter Green, Rory Gallagher, and Jerry Garcia showed up to gawk. Though the record with Polydor had been pulled, Zito was able to organize another studio session for Buchanan with local players and himself on drums featuring a selection of rock and blues covers, but it, too, was deemed unworthy of his incredible ability in live performance. More intriguing, Zito would later claim to have organized a session in Georgia with the Allman Brothers, at Duane's request, that Buchanan blew off, as he would to his detriment so many times throughout his career.

THE WORLD'S GREATEST UNKNOWN GUITAR PLAYER

Buchanan's increasing notoriety at the Crossroads compelled Denver to share more of the spotlight as two New Yorkers would step forward to sing his praises to a far larger audience. Part-time writer and amateur guitarist Bob Berman had heard of Buchanan in the 1960s from a professional guitarist friend and, after reading the *Rolling Stone* story, drove to the Crossroads. He, too, was stunned and interviewed him for *Guitar Player*. The *Rolling Stone* story also came to the attention of John Adams at WNET, the PBS-TV station in New York City, and he likewise made the long trek south to see Buchanan, was blown away, and wanted to make a documentary. It would eventually take seeing Buchanan at a special gig set up by Zito at Georgetown University in Washington to convince the brass at WNET to green light the project. The resultant film, often erroneously and inaccurately referred to as *The World's Greatest Unknown Guitar Player*, as he had been playing regularly in the US and even Japan since the late 1950s, is actually titled *Introducing Roy Buchanan* and ranges from a revealing reunion with his family in Pixley to numerous sections of him playing spectacularly in a variety of situations. Included is a jazzy version of "Misty" that composer Erroll Garner admired, and it captures him at the "crossroads" of his career, just before he went from the low, familial glow of cult status to the cold world of record company commercial pressure.

Buchanan finally quit Danny Denver after playing behind him, on and off, since 1964 and was awarded his own gig at the Crossroads. So would begin his questionable habit of surrounding himself with musicians whom he felt comfortable being around, but were not of his caliber, with few exceptions. One of those in his first band was future fellow virtuoso Danny Gatton, who came in on bass and was promoted to second lead guitar before he left to try to exploit his exceptional technique and become a rival with Buchanan. Years later, Buchanan would call the clubs where Gatton was booked and insist on the phone being left off the hook so he could hear what his competition was playing. The group stayed together long enough to have crazy Cajun fiddler Doug Kershaw sit in one night and for Buchanan to insult Leon Russell, who likewise wanted to come by and sit in but was rebuffed. Minus Gatton, they fortunately preserved some of the magic that could occur onstage with their live recording at the Crossroads titled *Buch and the Snakestretchers* (1971), which Buchanan had wished Polydor to release instead of the Charlie Daniels produced disk. Instead, he ended up putting the vinyl out on his B.I.O.Y.A (Blow It Out Your Ass) label in a burlap bag (released on CD in 1992 on the Genes label). Not amused, Polydor saw it as a violation of contract and initiated a lawsuit.

Concurrently, surprisingly enthusiastic response to the release of the WNET special would prove the upward tipping point for Buchanan, and it was purportedly their most requested broadcast. For a while, life continued as before, with a modest raise at his five sets/six-nights-a-week gig at My Mother's Place in upscale Georgetown, in addition to more amphetamines slugged down with Carling Black Label beer. But, by early 1972, the offers for concerts rather than clubs started pouring in, including one to play Carnegie Hall in New York City in early summer with his rough and tumble Snakestretchers. Hip to the buzz, Polydor soon came calling for their album with a producer who played guitar and banjo and was enthusiastic to record Buchanan. The guitarist and his flunkies, leery of corporate "suits," were resistant and prepared to play hardball until Polydor issued Buchanan a summons to appear in court for violating his contract. An accommodation was reached: "Buch," with the Snakestretchers, would come to New York for only two days to record his music, his way. *Roy Buchanan* would end up being little more than the Snakestretchers playing their typical bar room set. The liner photo showed a scruffy bunch who looked like Confederate soldiers from a Civil War photo. Included on the vinyl platter was Buchanan "stretching" on two extended instrumental blues jams, a "chicken pickin' instrumental and two future classics: his original "The Messiah Will Come Again," which he introduced with a "sermon," and his classic instrumental version of the Patsy Cline hit "Sweet Dreams." Chuck Tilley sang credibly on three country classics. The reviews were mixed, to say the least, but sales were encouraging and plans were made to get Buchanan back in the studio for another try in 1973.

THE POLYDOR YEARS

With Buchanan now more relaxed about coming to NYC and recording for Polydor, and the label having a better idea of how to present him, *Second Album* was an artistic triumph. Arguably his more representative and best record, it went gold and is considered a classic. Mostly instrumental blues and country ballads, it contains perhaps his definitive version of "After Hours," as well as the heart wrenching, melancholy Buchanan originals "Five String Blues" and "I Won't Tell You No Lies." The sales were good and reviews were uniformly positive in varying degrees, but the execs at Polydor could see that he was not going to be the big star they has envisioned. The third release, *That's What I'm Here For*, thrown together in 1973, was an attempt at expanding beyond the bar band repertoire, with a desire to score vocal hits. "Hey Joe" and "Roy's Bluz," from his standard live set and both "sung" by Buchanan, were surrounded by blue eyed soul and, perhaps, too many country tunes spotlighting a new singer in the excellent Billy Price. The reviews were not as good for the eclectic mix of material, *Guitar Player* magazine being an exception, and several panned Buchanan for exhibiting too much flash, as evidenced by the bombast on "Hey Joe." In addition, during the recording sessions, Buchanan, in his usual way of sabotaging himself, blew off a chance to record with John Lennon, who was bending over backwards to accommodate the guitarist.

By the middle of 1974, Buchanan and band were in California to cut *In the Beginning* (#160), with more R&B covers promoting soul shouter Billy Sheffield, along with a smattering of originals, some blues and three moody instrumentals that, along with the blues, would always be the high points of his recorded output. With disappointing but unsurprising tepid sales, it was agreed, through personal manager Jay Reich's negotiating, to have Buchanan fulfill the remaining obligation on his contract with Polydor with a live album recorded at Town Hall in NYC with singer Billy Price back in front of the band. *Livestock* was a bit restrained compared to his best live gigs going down at that time, but still ranks high in the canon. The quality performances and eclectic selection of songs worked well, despite some of them having been arranged on the spot, as had haphazardly occurred with the studio albums. The version of "Further on Up the Road" was "stolen" by Eric Clapton after he was given a tape of the show by the producer and would come to irritate Buchanan. However, he may have forgotten how he had been highly influenced by the Ronnie Hawkins version from 1961.

THE ATLANTIC YEARS

With a far more significant advance, the blessing of legendary Atlantic Records mogul Ahmet Ertegun, and the legendary Tom Dowd slated to produce, Buchanan and company prepared to track the first of three albums for the label in 1975. *A Street Called Straight* (#148) immediately got off on the wrong foot when Ertegun insisted on using his producer, Arif Mardin, instead of Dowd. One can only fantasize about what the results would have been with the heavy blues-rock expert in charge. Weighted down with having to sing lead and freak out on guitar, in addition to having the jazzy horns of the Brecker Brothers, backup singers, extra studio cats, and a glossy production more suitable to the slick black pop and disco music of the era, overwhelmed Buchanan and what the basic band did best. Such was his talent, however, that he could still stand out of the mash up of styles with "My Friend Jeff," a hard rocking instrumental tribute to Jeff Beck in acknowledgement of the British guitarist's dedication of "Cause We've Ended as Lovers" to his American counterpart, and a vocal/instrumental cover of Hendrix' hippie anthem "If Six was Nine." More typical, however, was the horror movie sound effects of "Guitar Cadenza" and the overwrought and maudlin country weepers "Caruso" and "I Still Think About Ida Mae." If more evidence was needed for the lack of a coherent vision, yet another version of "The Messiah Will Come Again" was included with superfluous synthesizers. Included in the rough mix was the soulful "Good God Have Mercy," penned expressly for Buchanan by Billy Roberts, the composer of "Hey Joe." Nonetheless, the reviews were encouraging from critics who were likely happy to hear some conventional vocal songs they could grasp, instead of virtuosic guitar jams.

Loading Zone (#105), in 1977, was an intriguing if questionable attempt to capitalize on Buchanan's strengths in a fusion/blues context. With Tom Dowd again not invited to the party, jazz-rock bass star Stanley Clarke was brought in to push Buchanan out of his "comfort zone" and, except for keyboardist Malcolm Lukens, the touring band was left out. Again, the results were ambiguous, with the most successful cuts being the heavy guitar of "Ramon's Blues" and an epic "Green Onions," both with Steve Cropper contributing his impressive Tele chops, and the barroom shuffle blues "Done Your Daddy Dirty." Several ethereal compositions could not have been more out of place. However, a rockabilly duet with Clarke, who chose the questionable title for "Adventures of Brer Rabbit and Tar Baby," showed that Buchanan could still "pick the chicken." But the lack of commercial success meant heads had to roll, and his longtime personal manager, Jay Reich, who had tried so hard to do right by his eccentric artist, was the first to feel the cut, followed by select band members.

You Are Not Alone (#119) completed his obligation to Atlantic in 1978, and both artist and record company must have given a rueful sigh of relief. The album cover, with a passé space age rendering on the front and a photo on the back showing a Les Paul Special, should have been the tip-off that the wheels had come completely off. Though there was the obligatory blues jam with the typical "1841 Shuffle" for those who longed for the early Polydor years and a tasty excursion on Neil Young's "Down by the River," the rest were either spacey meanderings or pounding 1970s arena rock. True to form, the final hit-and-miss affair had nowhere near the critical or commercial impact originally imagined by Ertegun three years earlier.

FADING AWAY

Totally disillusioned with the record business and abusing alcohol and drugs to an even greater degree, Buchanan retreated back into his world of playing gigs when they came along. With Judy Buchanan now managing her husband, new backup bands were put in place and the road beckoned. In the early 1980s, Buchanan made two critical changes: He retired his prized '53 Tele, supposedly after Danny Gatton changed a pot and altered its iconic sound, and he switched to a Strat. Plus, he began appearing onstage loaded to the point that it affected his performance—something he had never done in the past. Most telling and disturbing was an incident that occurred in 1980 near his Virginia home where he was arrested, beaten by the cops, and apparently tried to hang himself in his jail cell.

On the rebound, Buchanan threw a band together, secured recording time at the Record Plant in NYC, arrived with scant material, and self-produced *My Babe* (#193) in two days. A selection of mostly originals written by him and lead singer Paul Jacobs, with a few chestnuts thrown in, it got surprisingly good reviews for the most part and even earned a shout out from *Billboard* as a "breakout" album in the midst of the New Wave craze. Functioning modestly as a "comeback" of sorts, it seemed to rejuvenate Buchanan, and he went back out on the road, including a tour in Australia. However, by 1982, he had jettisoned his band and would begin using pickup musicians and doing one-nighters booked by Judy. When he finally settled on some regulars, they all indulged in massive amounts of cocaine while still managing to perform, despite the leader's deteriorating mental and physical condition. In 1984, Jay Reich was invited back in to make personnel changes and to stop Buchanan from "going down slow."

THE ALLIGATOR YEARS

The year 1984 would significantly mark the beginning of his second act and also the final chapter in a life overburdened by talent and the promise of great rewards that it entailed. While playing a gig in Toronto and sober for a change, Buchanan was heard by Bruce Iglauer, president of Alligator Records, the premier independent blues label. The chance encounter led to a contract that would produce some of his finest recordings after the earliest Polydor disks. With world renowned producer, blues scholar, and writer Dick Shurman onboard, it was the perfect marriage of Buchanan's extraordinary ability meeting the enablers to give him the freedom in the studio that he always desired. With Buchanan playing new Teles sporting Bill Lawrence pickups, a group of choice Chicago musicians augmented by guest vocalists, and a selection of instrumentals, including "Chicago Smokeshop" and "Short Fuse," as well as prime covers, *When a Guitar Plays the Blues* (#162), released in 1985, was an unqualified success by any yardstick. It was even nominated for a Grammy as Blues Album of the Year. The artist, label, critics, and fans were all in a positive frame of mind. In addition, Buchanan was now gigging within a power trio context, with a young bassist and drummer, that was the proper fit for a more commercial, harder rocking direction. A highlight occurred with a show at Carnegie Hall at the end of the year called *American Guitar Heroes* with Albert Collins and Lonnie Mack, though he was required to use two new backing musicians due to union rules. Unfortunately, amongst the positive aspect of his career at this juncture, Buchanan had begun slipping off the wagon again, as just one beer could lead him directly to heavier substances.

In 1986, Buchanan returned to Chicago for the unwittingly and ironically titled *Dancing on the Edge* (#153), which contained a new group of true blues backing musicians. With veteran Delbert McClinton taking two vocal turns and a volcanic version of "Peter Gunn" among other instrumentals and vocal tracks by Buchanan, it was another step forward in the evolution of his new sound and approach. In 1987, true to form, he again grabbed his burgeoning bag of old cassettes with song snippets and went back to Chicago with a Les Paul Custom (instead of a Tele) to record *Hot Wires* with the same backing band that he had enjoyed working with previously. Unfortunately, during the recording process, it became obvious that he was back to his old habits away from the studio, though his solos were just as blistering as in the past.

ROY'S BLUES

The year 1988 started out with an extremely ambitious touring schedule, with his trio routed to take Buchanan through to late summer, after which he would take a break and then resume touring in support of *Hot Wires*. He expressed the desire to renew his contract with Alligator and commence work on a fourth album in the fall. Califonia luthier Roger Fritz proposed a series of Roy Buchanan signature guitars based on the Tele, beginning with the Bluesmaster Model. In late July, he showed up for a gig in Connecticut with his head shaved and strict orders from his doctor not to drink alcohol with the antidepressant pills that he was taking. Nonetheless, his contract rider specified two cases of beer, as usual. At the outdoor show with Matt "Guitar" Murphy dubbed "Guitar Wars," he rocked hard like a man possessed, basked in the adulation of the ecstatic crowd, partied, and headed home to Reston, Virginia, for a couple of weeks off to cool down. But on Sunday, August 14, it all came to a tragic end. Buchanan started drinking in the afternoon, and after coming home drunk in the evening with a stranger whose demeanor alarmed Judy, he left on foot without saying where he was going, following down the street the stranger, who was driving slowly away with his lights off. What happened next has been the subject of intense debate and remains unresolved. Buchanan was arrested for public drunkenness and during the night either hung himself in his cell or was the victim of police brutality. Those who knew him were divided on whether the hellhounds had finally caught up to his trail, or if there was a police cover up in the murder of a national cultural treasure. He was 48 years old.

Fortunately, Roy Buchanan left a rich legacy of recorded music and film. As with Hendrix, no torch was passed, just the inspiration to countless guitarists to listen and learn from a master who will never be replaced.

GEAR

Like the stories Buchanan notoriously told to mythologize his life, the chronology of his guitars is fraught with seemingly unverifiable facts. The best available information to date is as follows: Besides "Nancy," his famed 1953 Tele, Buchanan also used 1954 and 1955 models on the Polydor albums. Typically, he played through either a pre-CBS blackface or a CBS silverface Fender Vibrolux with two 10" speakers. The Atlantic albums feature his Martin D-28, as well as a late-1950s' Les Paul Special.

He also began using a pre-CBS Strat in the early 1980s. In 1985, he switched to a 1983 Tele with Bill Lawrence pickups and a 30th Anniversary Gibson Les Paul Goldtop. The photo on the cover of Phil Carson's book seems to confirm that he also tried various Guild Tele-style guitars with EMG pickups and a pointy headstock, but was dissatisfied with them. By 1988, he was playing a signature model Fritz Brothers Tele-style Bluesmaster with three EMG pickups through a Roland JC-120 amp.

Buchanan said in a *Guitar Player* interview that he used Fender Rock 'n' Roll strings (.010–.038), but Seymour Duncan claimed "Nancy" had .009–.046 gauges when he examined her. It is agreed that he would buy "10" sets and swap out the .010 high E for a .009. For most of his career, he studiously avoided stomp box effects but, around 1984, he started incorporating a Boss DD-2 delay pedal.

AFTER HOURS

(*Second Album*, 1973)
Music by Avery Parrish
Words by Robert Bruce and Buddy Feyne

The Erskine Hawkins Orchestra recorded the first version of the future Avery Parrish immortal slow blues in 1940, featuring Parrish on piano. It would become so popular and ubiquitous in the community as to be affectionately called the "black national anthem." Buchanan was significantly inspired by the Jimmy Nolen version, but took his interpretation to a place unimagined by virtually any other blues guitarist and created a masterpiece for all time.

Figure 1—Section B

His first 12-bar chorus of blues with the "fast change" shows Buchanan packing in more soul and drama than most guitarists could in 48 measures or more. In measures 1 and 2, over the I (G7) and IV (C7) chords, respectively, he plays a credible reproduction of the original piano part with triads and dyads before jumping into his unique vision of the blues. Mining the G minor pentatonic scale for sparkling gems in the root position and the "Albert King box," Buchanan negotiates the chord changes with classic and sublime note choices. These include regularly resolving to the root notes of the I, IV, and V (D7) chords and producing tart tension with numerous slinky bends. A favorite of the Tele-man is the whole-step bend from the root (C) to the 9th (D), as seen in measures 2 and 5 over the IV chord. Observe the tantalizingly slow multi-step bend in measure 5 that contains the G (5th) briefly inserted before it is released. In addition, check out how the same bend of C to D functions as the 4th to the 5th in measures 7 and 8 over the I chord.

Performance Tip: Execute the too cool, quarter-step bends to the "true blue note" in between the ♭3rd (B♭) and 3rd (B) with the index finger in measures 3, 7, and 12.

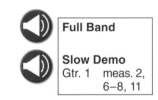

Full Band

Slow Demo
Gtr. 1   meas. 2,
6–8, 11

Fig. 1

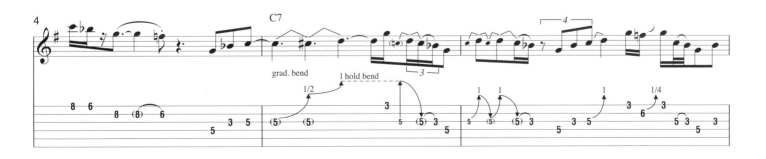

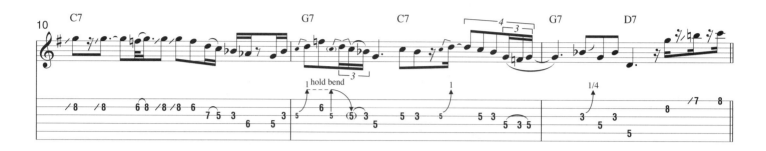

Figure 2—Section C

Buchanan throws down the gauntlet to any and all six-string challengers in measures 1–2 with a blur of rapid-fire strums on the C bent to D before it is gradually released on beats 3 and 4 over the IV chord (C7) for eventual resolution. The galvanizing effect of the maneuver is breathtaking to behold and is only topped by measures 3–4 over the I chord (G7) that follows, where he twists and turns his dynamic phrasing with taut note clusters, percussive mutes, and startling bends and releases that sound like a horse whinnying. In measures 5–7, over the IV–I changes, he offers a glimpse of his unparalleled string bending technique with a slippery sequence phrased in a profoundly vocal manner. One other point of interest out of many occurs in measures 9–10, where Buchanan bends the root (D) to the 2nd (E) over the V chord and the ♭5th (F#/G♭) to the to the 5th (G) over the IV chord in an example of his penchant to go outside the minor pentatonic scale when it suits his tastes.

Performance Tip: Bend the C to D in measures 1–2 with the ring finger, backed up by the middle and index.

Fig. 2

Full Band

Slow Demo
Gtr. 1   meas. 1,
           3–5, 10–11

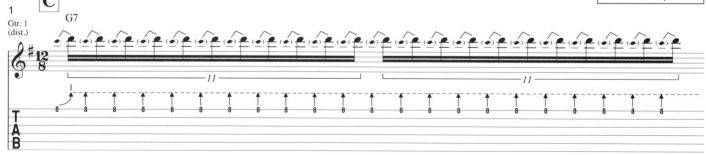

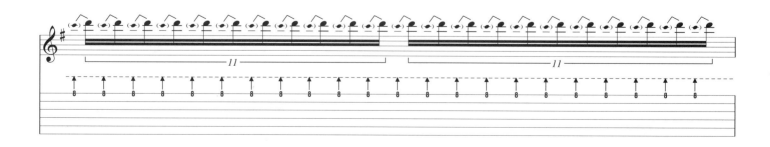

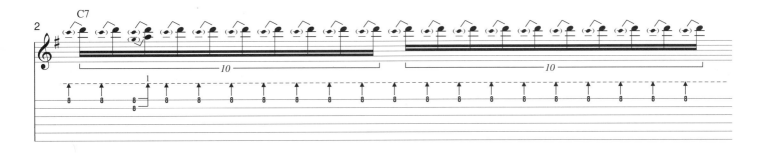

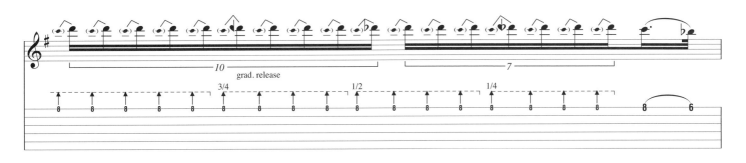

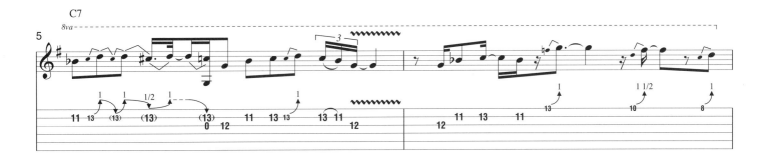

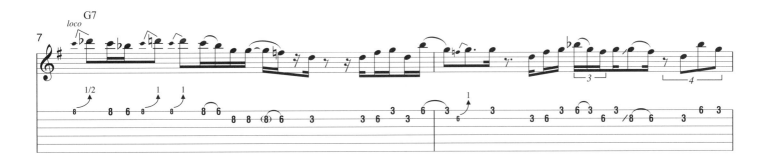

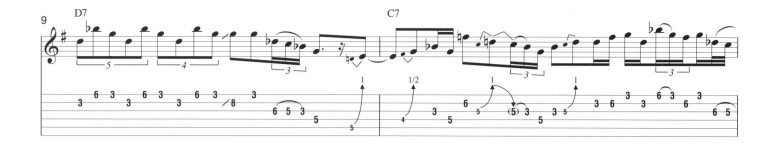

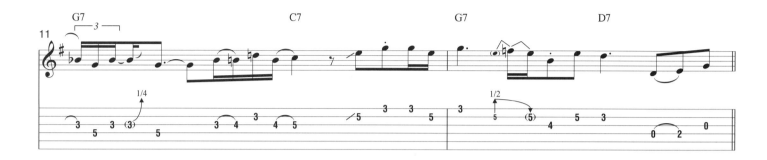

Figure 3—Section F

Remaining with the warm neck pickup on his Tele following the switch in Section E (not shown), Buchanan gives an object lesson in low volume, nuanced blues soloing that one rarely, if ever, hears in electric blues guitar these days. Virtually every measure contains a new melodic, rhythmic, or dynamic improvisational idea, with one leading fluidly to the next. Measures 1 and 2, over the I (G7) and IV (C7) chords, set the table for the appetizing musical feast for the ears that follows with the spicy ♭5th (D♭) for tension and the consonant 3rd (E), respectively. From there on through to measure 9, over the V chord (D7), Buchanan serves up sweet morsels around the 12th position in a less frequently used "blues box." The advantage to this soloing strategy is the easy access to the root notes of the I and IV chords at fret 12 on string 3 and at fret 13 on string 2, respectively, along with the all-important B♭ (functioning as the ♭3rd in G or ♭7th in C) at fret 11 on string 2. In addition, a multitude of bends, his specialty, is available from both notes, resulting in a sublime vocal effect that is especially expressive in measures 7–8, over the I chord.

Relocating at last to "home base" in the root position of the G minor pentatonic scale (at fret 3) in measures 9 and 10, over the V and IV changes, Buchanan swings the rhythm in a gently descending line that leads seamlessly to the turnaround in measures 11–12. The triads, dyads, and triple-stops in the former brilliantly convey the harmony of the I and IV chords, while single notes and dyads do the same for the I and V in the latter, with the rich, satisfying harmony providing the perfect conclusion.

Performance Tip: The bends in measures 7–8 should be executed with the ring (fret 13) and index (fret 11) fingers.

Full Band

Slow Demo
Gtr. 1   meas. 11–12

Fig. 3

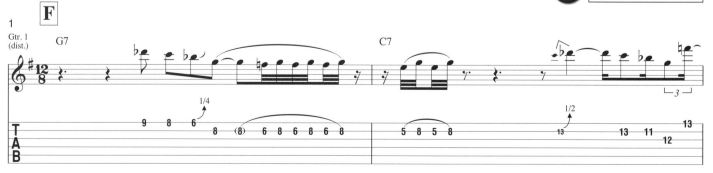

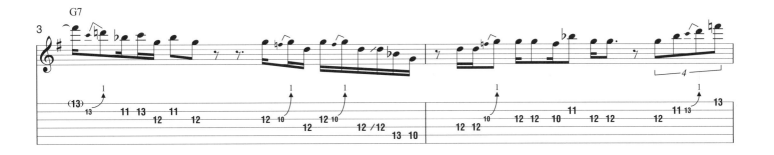

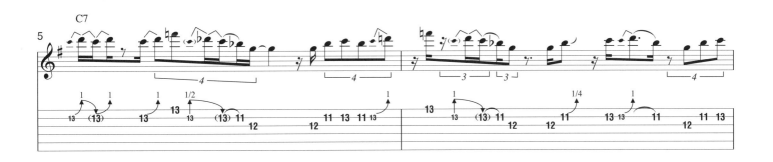

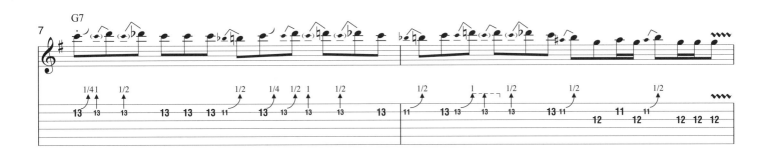

AFTER HOURS

19

Figure 4—Section H

In his last 12-bar chorus, Buchanan opts to resist going out with a big bang and instead stays on the "down low" with gorgeous, silky smooth, dreamy harmonies supported by his patented volume swells. Calling on his authentic knowledge of steel guitar technique, he bends dyads and single notes with uncommon lyricism. Observe the raked broken chords ending with the 3rd bent a half step to the suspended 4th for tension, relative to the I (G7) and IV (C7) chords, in measures 1 and 2. The G7 triple stop in measure 8 over the I chord is only one highlight among an entire chorus of spectacular moves. Be sure not to miss the sequence in measures 3–7, where he uses bent dyads and related single notes to navigate the I–IV–I changes in a glorious flow of honey-flavored 3rds.

In measure 9, dyads in 6ths relative to the V chord and similar to those employed in "Honky Tonk" begin the transition to the turnaround, following the C bebop dominant scale licks in measure 10, over the IV chord. Buchanan then wraps it all up with classic licks that outline the changes beautifully, reminiscent of Freddie King and Hendrix in the final, ending turnaround from his studio version of "Red House." Check out how the logical and melodic lines outline the changes while also ascending to a climax and resolution in measure 12. Seeming to not want to end his epic "case of the blues," Buchanan plays a coda in free time in the root octave position of the G minor pentatonic scale with the intelligent addition of the 9th (A) bent a full step to the major tonality-defining 3rd (B), followed by the root (G). Perfecto! (Note: Buchanan liked cigars.)

Performance Tip: The best way to play the licks in measures 1, 2, 6, and 8 is to form E string barre chords at frets 3, 8, 3, and 3, respectively, and only pick the notes presented.

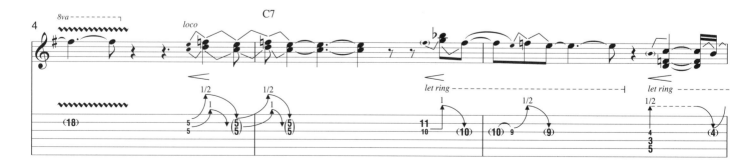

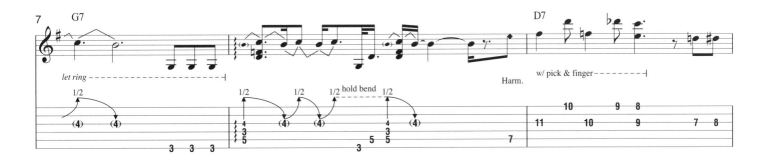

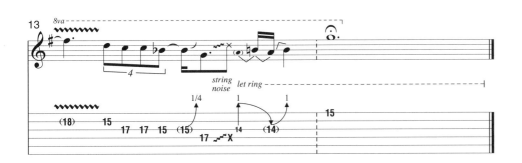

CHICAGO SMOKESHOP

(*When a Guitar Plays the Blues*, 1985)
Written by Roy Buchanan

The first album for Alligator was a sign of a new beginning for Buchanan and a microcosm of what had gone before: A few laconic vocals by the reticent artist, a couple of excellent guest singers, and a handful of instrumentals as the high points. "Chicago Smokeshop," with the great, unsung Chicago blues and gospel guitarist Criss Johnson on rhythm guitar, is a scorching example of the latter and was named for a favorite tobacco emporium in the Windy City. The change in guitars, resulting in a cleaner, brighter, steely sound as opposed to the rich, warm distortion of the Polydor years, particularly, is quite noticeable, but seems to have been what Buchanan desired at that point.

Figure 5—Intro (Section A)

Criss Johnson (Gtr. 1) utilizes standard, blues-based boogie patterns with 5ths, 6ths, and ♭7ths, along with 4ths and 3rds for the I (E7) change in a most uncommon way. The result is a Middle Eastern melody that was used for a children's song about "The girls in France…" If one uses a little imagination, the riff from the Isley Brothers' "It's Your Thing" also comes to mind. Johnson then harmonizes similar patterns to follow for the I, IV (A7), and V (B7) changes in the various rehearsal sections (not shown).

Performance Tip: If the pinky is used to access the D (♭7th) at fret 5 on string 5, add the ring finger for the F♯ (2nd) at fret 4 on string 4 in measures 2 and 4.

Full Band

Slow Demo
Gtr. 1 meas. 1

Fig. 5

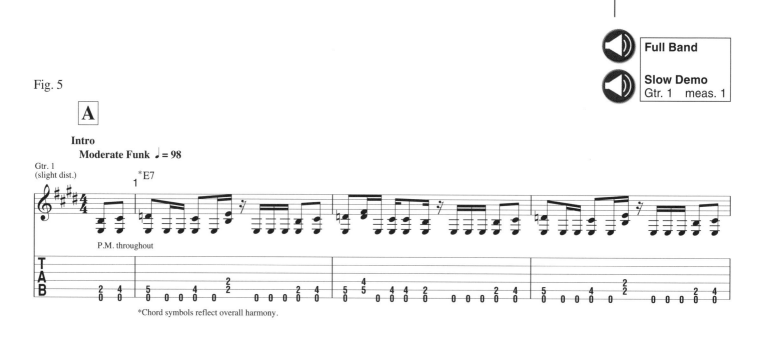

*Chord symbols reflect overall harmony.

Figure 6—Section C

Buchanan (Gtr. 2) pays respectful tribute to Buddy Guy, one of the legends of Chicago blues guitar, with riffs similar to "Buddy's Blues" and "Strange Brew," as co-written and recorded by Eric Clapton when he was with Cream in the late 1960s. Significant is the way the four-measure motif emphasizing the E tonality repeats twice while harmonizing with the I (E7), IV (A7), and I chords in measures 1–8 of the 12-bar progression with the "slow change." Additionally, a variation on the basic theme is incorporated in measures 9–12, over the V (B7), IV, and I chords, to complete a memorable "head," even though it occurs in Section C instead of earlier in B or A.

Performance Tip: The classic unison bend (D to E) in the octave position of the E minor pentatonic scale that crosses the bar line, from measure 4 to 5, should be played with the index holding down the E at fret 12 on string 1 while the pinky, backed up by the ring and middle fingers, does the bending at fret 15 on string 2.

Fig. 6

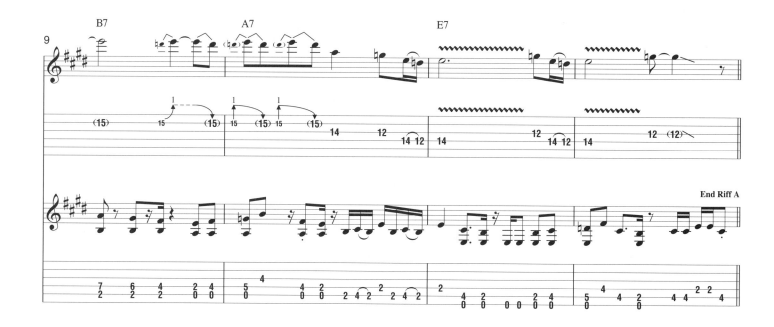

Figure 7—Section E

Given the space to stretch out and take his time, Buchanan was unexcelled at building musical tension. In Section E, his natural sense of instrumental composition comes into play as he starts off with long, bent and released, sustained, and vibratoed notes in the lower register of the E minor pentatonic scale during measures 1–4, over the I chord (E7). In conclusion, in measures 9 and 10 over the V (B7) and IV (A7) chords, he descends in a similar fashion from around the octave, but with the urgency of more notes and bends to increase the musical tension before resolving with root (E) notes in measures 11–12, over the I chord. In between, over the IV and I chords, in shades of his early rock 'n' roll days, he contrasts repetitive bluesy dyads, classic Chuck Berry-style riffs, and numerous hits to the E note in the octave position of the E minor pentatonic scale. The result turns up the heat for the high point in the middle of the 12-bar section.

Performance Tip: The middle finger, backed by the index, should be used for the bends in measures 1–3 and 10, while the pinky, backed by the ring, middle, and index fingers, will be more efficient on strings 2 and 1 in measures 4 and 9.

Full Band

Slow Demo
Gtr. 2   meas. 5–6,
8, 11

Fig. 7

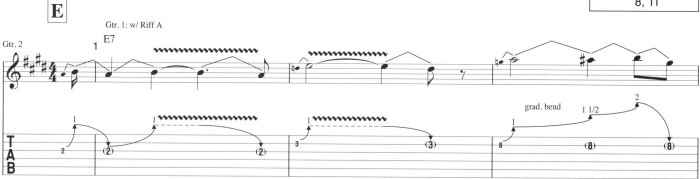

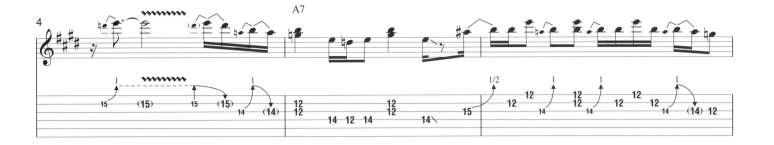

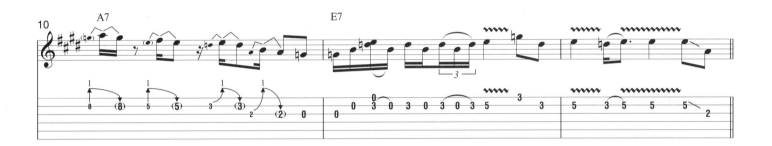

Figure 8—Section H

In Sections H–J, Buchanan just annihilates the strings on his Tele in an overwhelming barrage of machine gun notes, torturous bends, and assorted squeaks and sqawks before utilizing Section K (not shown) as a virtual reprise of Section C. Section H suffices as an excellent overview of the way he is able to harness his seemingly bottomless well of improvisation tools into a coherent musical statement. He begins innocently enough in the octave position of the E minor pentatonic scale in measures 1–2, over the I (E7), by pummeling the root note straight on and bent from the ♭7th (D) on string 2 at fret 15, albeit at sub-supersonic speed. However, once he reaches measure 3, he breaks through the sound barrier up to measure 9 with cluster bombs of stunningly syncopated 16th and 32nd notes. Notice the subtle nuance of his inclusion of the F♯, D♯, and C♯ notes in measures 4, 5, and 6, respectively, from the hip bebop dominant scale. Surprisingly, Buchanan accomplishes his impressive feat by picking long, connected horizontal skeins in graceful arcs, rather than by riffing intensely up and down in vertical boxes.

Always the sly bluesman, he anticipates measures 11–12 (I chord) by commencing to ramp down the atomic energy in measures 9 and 10, over the V (B7) and IV (A7) chords, with attention to the E note, functioning as the 4th and 5th, respectively. The deliberate tension created is resolved logically in measure 12 with the root (E) note, following another shot of tangy tension courtesy of the 4th (A) bent to the 5th (B) in measure 11.

Performance Tip: Alternate down and up pick strokes are a necessity in order to efficiently play the fast single-note lines.

Fig. 8

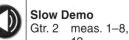
H

Gtr. 1: w/ Riff A

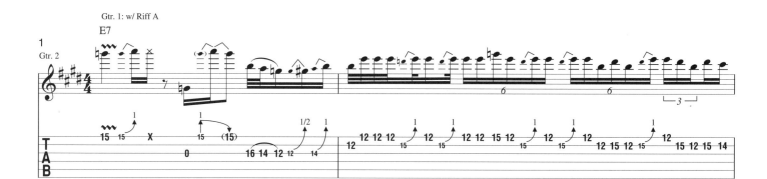

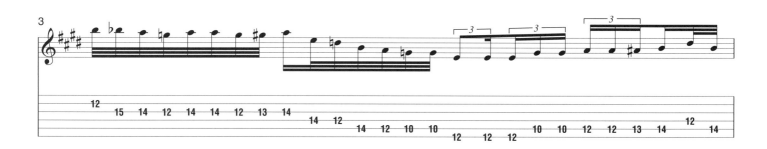

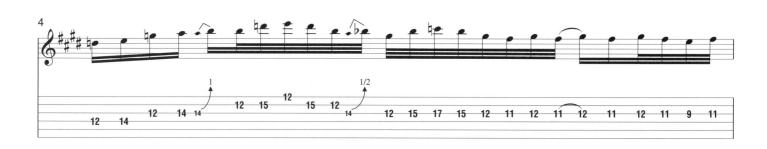

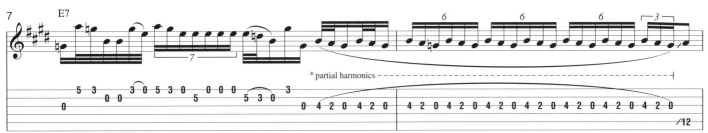

*Lightly touch string 3 with side of right-hand pinky and slide towards bridge while slurring.

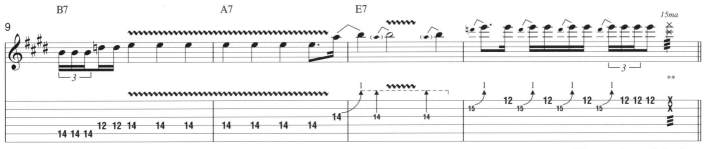

** Press on strings past fretboard, near bridge pickup, and gradually slide towards neck while tremolo picking.

FIVE STRING BLUES

(*Second Album*, 1973)

By Roy Buchanan

This is possibly the most emotionally devastating blues from a guitarist whose ability to directly and personally touch his audience in his best work even outweighs his virtuosity. It is arguably the most personal of his dramatic minor key compositions, which include "I Won't Tell You No Lies" and "The Messiah Will Come Again." The enigmatic title and spoken-word religious declaration in Section E (not shown) only contribute to the mystical power of the track.

Figure 9—Section B

Buchanan roams through the dark night of his soul in the D minor slow blues, using his mastery of the blues scale that was second to none. Through the amazingly expressive manipulation of his volume and tone controls in the first 12-bar blues chorus, he announces his intent to instrumentally plumb the depths of his emotions in the melancholy progression. Observe how he does not so much as navigate the chords with specific note selection, but responds to the function of each change relative to the flow of harmony. This can be heard in measure 5, over the iv chord (Gm), where he swoops from the root (G) to the 9th (A) to complement the forward motion of the progression from the i change (Dm). Likewise, he builds anticipation in measure 8, over the i chord, with stuttering, syncopated lines before releasing it in measure 9, over the VI chord (B♭), with fluid, multi-step bends à la Albert King that help define the major tonality via the 6th (G) and major 7th (A) notes. Further accentuating this critical juncture in the progression, Buchanan follows with harmony based around D/F (3rd/5th) double-stops, as often utilized by Buddy Guy.

Performance Tip: On Teles and Strats, curl the pinky finger around the volume and tone controls to play the swells and wah-wah effect, respectively.

Full Band

Slow Demo
Gtr. 1   meas. 6–12

Fig. 9

Slow Blues ♩. = 44

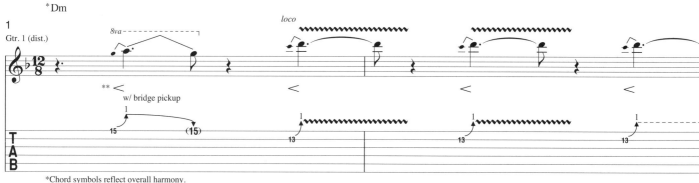

*Chord symbols reflect overall harmony.
**Volume swells throughout.

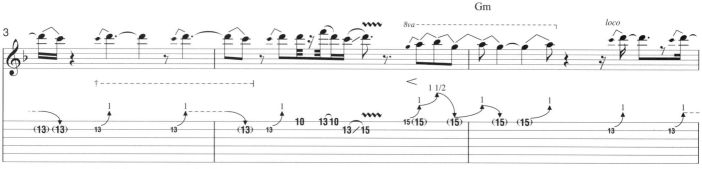

†Manipulate tone control on the guitar to create a wah-wah effect.

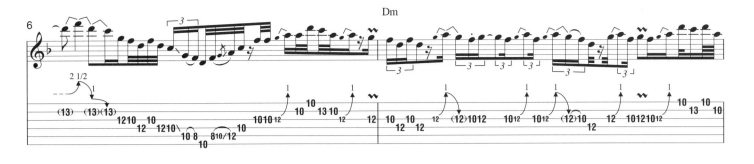

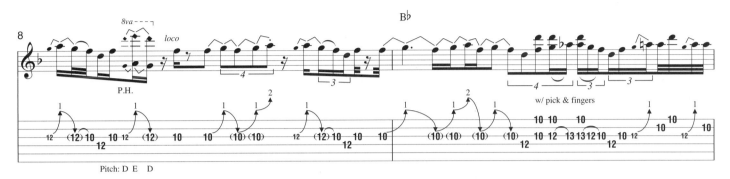

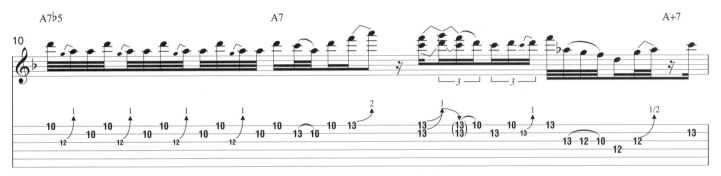

Figure 10—Section C

Buchanan immediately dials up the intensity level in the next 12-bar chorus with soaring bends, tightly-coiled repeating licks, and his trademark "backwards" phrasing. Check out how he takes a different tack in virtually every measure after coming in with squealing, high-register bends like a cry in the wilderness in measure 1, over the i chord (Dm). Beginning to build momentum, he plays 16th-note triplets in measure 2 that emphasize the root (D) note, followed by tense, reverse riffs in the same root-octave position of the D blues scale in measure 3 before hurtling down the "blues box" to pick up the pace again. Now on a roll, he accelerates by climbing back up the scale in measure 4 in dramatic, ascending 32nd-note increments that climax with breathtaking, multi-step bends and conclude with a bend from the ♭3rd (F) to the 4th (G) that anticipates the approaching change to the iv chord (Gm).

Sticking with the soloing strategy of ebb and flow in register, along with tension and release, Buchanan takes a circuitous path down the scale in measure 5, over the iv chord (Gm), with little acknowledgement of the root (G). He then whips into a classic repeating blues riff to lock in the tension that crosses the bar line into measure 6 and involves the root (G) bent to the 9th (A) and the 4th (C) pitched up a bluesy quarter step. Choosing yet another pathway to musical tension, he limits his rapt attention to the F, G, and D notes on strings 3 and 4, which represent the epicenter of traditional blues tonality, and crosses the bar line, repeating similar spiky licks into measure 7, over the i chord. Once ensconced back on the tonic chord, Buchanan endeavors to prove his exalted status among guitarists. Proceeding in measure 8 to brilliantly and dramatically build tantalizing anticipation to a jaw-dropping climax in measure 9, over the VI chord (B♭), he gradually adds more notes to his twisting, convoluted licks, while compressing musical space until he urgently arrives at the major tonality-defining 3rd (D) on beat 4. After briefly playing it on beat 1 of measure 9 to subtly push the action forward across the bar line, he again takes advantage of the natural, dissonant tension of the B♭ by repeatedly choking off the 5th (F) in a stunning display of how virtually one note at the right time can deliver a musical wallop, like a punch to the solar plexus.

Buchanan keeps pouring on the pathos in measure 10, over the V chords (A7♭5 and A7), with the tightly-compacted F, G, and D notes similar to measure 6, but prominently punctuated with dramatic, moaning bends of the ♭7th (G) to the root (A). And just when it seems that he may exceed across the invisible emotional line of blues angst, he resolves it all with fleet, punchy licks emphasizing the root (D) note in measures 11–12, over the i chord.

Performance Tip: In measure 8, play the classic harmony bend by holding the G bent to A on string 3 with the ring finger, backed up by the middle and index fingers, while simultaneously adding the F on top with the pinky.

Full Band

Slow Demo
Gtr. 1   meas. 2–12

Fig. 10

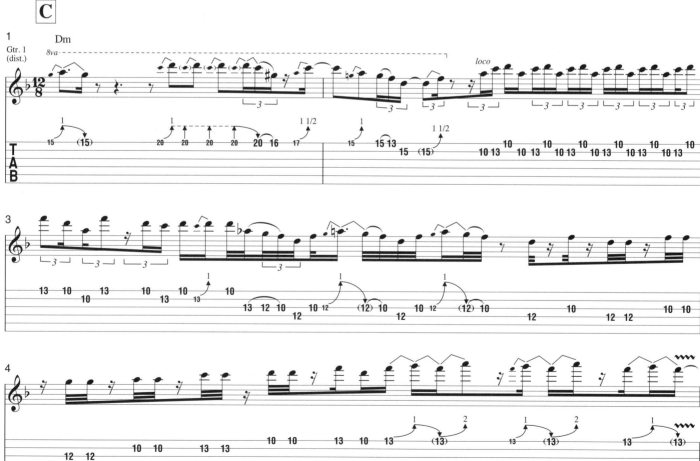

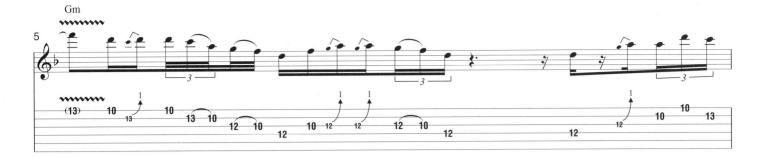

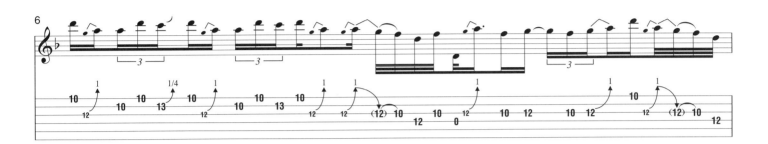

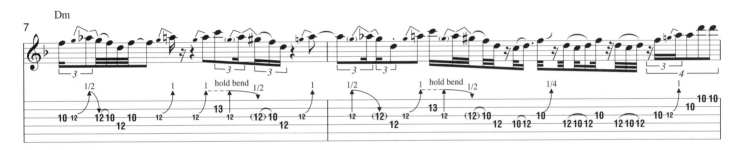

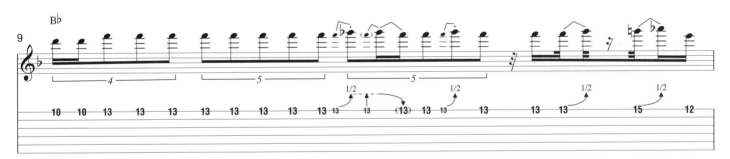

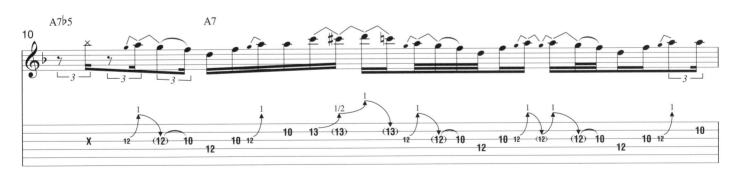

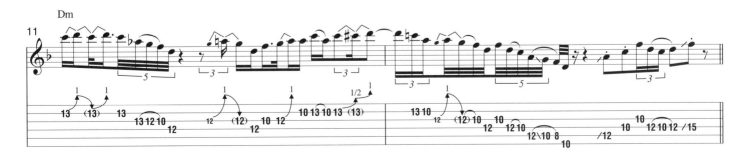

Figure 11—Section G

Buchanan saved his best shot for last in his epic minor blues that fades out during measure 10. Through to measure 9, over the VI chord (B♭), he twists his tone knob in conjunction with executing a veritable endless variety of bends to produce a crying, wah-wah effect that may well have been the sum total of his lifetime of grief to that point. Observe how his sound has more of an organic, natural quality than even the most advanced wah-wah pedals. It is a combination of eliminating the tone-sucking stomp box by going straight from the guitar to the amp, along with the critical component of the artist's extraordinary sensitivity to touch, tone, and phrasing. As in measure 9 of Section C (Fig. 10), though not as radically, Buchanan employs a limited palette, using the C note on string 2 at fret 13 as his basis.

The secret to his phenomenal expression, of course, is his virtuosic string manipulation. Ranging from one step to D (root over the i chord, 5th over the iv chord), one and a half steps to E♭ (♭9th of i), two steps to E (9th and 13th, respectively), and two and a half steps to F (♭3rd and ♭7th, respectively), it is the epitome of instrumental vocalizing created by bent strings and bass to treble tone manipulation. In measure 8, over the i chord, he eases out of the wah phase of the solo as the fade advances and continues with aggressive string bending and "whistling" pinch harmonics in a manner that suggests he is not going "quietly into the dark night." Measures 9 and 10, over the VI and V7 chords, respectively, though reduced in volume considerably, find him still striking sparks with the aforementioned classic blues licks, producing stinging tension in the former and, in the latter, spiraling licks emphasizing the root (A) for resolution in the root-octave position of the D minor pentatonic scale.

Performance Tip: By bending the C note with the pinky, backed up by the ring, middle, and index fingers, the left hand will be in an advantageous position to access other notes in the root-octave D minor pentatonic scale.

Full Band

Slow Demo
Gtr. 1   meas. 8–10

Fig. 11

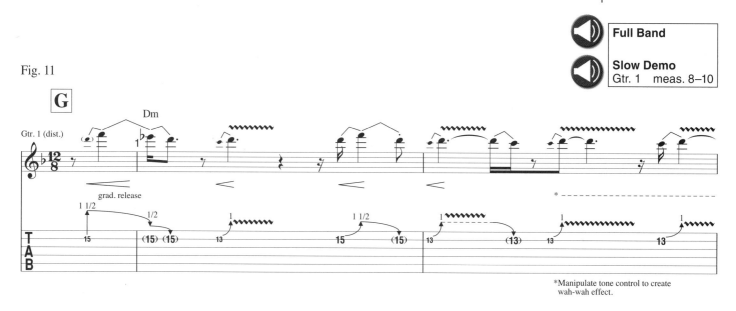

*Manipulate tone control to create wah-wah effect.

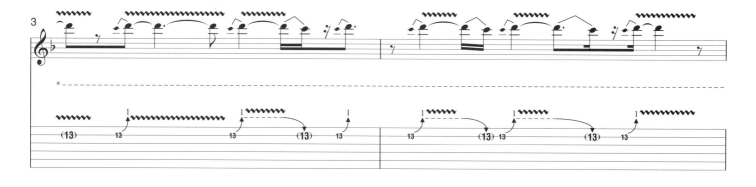

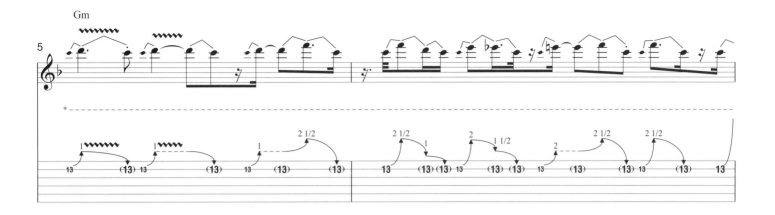

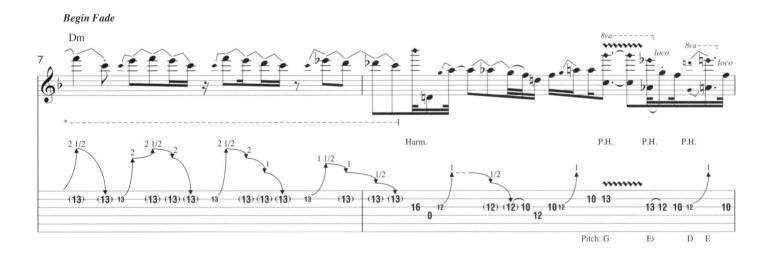

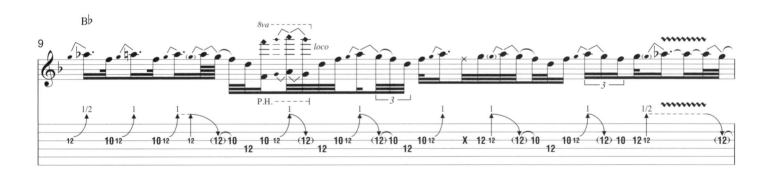

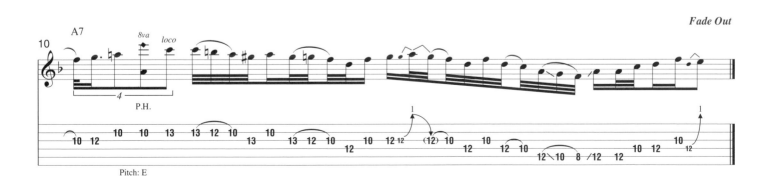

HEY JOE

(*Sweet Dreams: The Anthology*, 1992)
Words and Music by Billy Roberts

Buchanan uncorked one of the fiercest versions of this staple from his shows while on tour in Japan in June 1977. The man himself said the resulting album, *Live in Japan*, originally released overseas only in 1978, was his favorite. Hugely dramatic, with unleashed musical aggression appropriate to the lyrical content, it is tempting to see "Hey Joe" as a literal expression of the dark side of his soul.

Figure 12—Intro

Immediately placing his individual stamp on the classic rock ballad, Buchanan plays rumbling, distorted chords punctuated with knife-like runs in the first eight measures that precede the two eight-bar instrumental verses that follow. The wide range of his musical expression within the span of 24 measures is all the more remarkable for his relying on creativity rather than virtuosic technique. In measures 1–3, he ascends chromatically and dramatically with barre chords from G7 (♭III) to B7 (V), in sync with his keyboardist on organ, in an effective build up that he similarly employed on various slow blues.

Unaccompanied in measures 4–7, over the I chord (E), he rifles through the E minor pentatonic scale with quick hits on E major voicings to fill out this section with harmony, while ending on a big, nasty sounding open position E/G♯ in first inversion. Measures 9–16 reharmonize the verse with ♭VI (C/G), ♭III (G and Gsus2/F♯), and IV(Asus4) chords, followed by an improvised take on the famous Hendrix bass figure in measures 13–14 that leads to raspy, bluesy licks as the band enters. In measures 17–24, Buchanan dynamically and abruptly changes to clean, low-volume, and delicate riffing that skips and dances up to his first vocal verse (not shown).

Performance Tip: Play the E/G♯ chord, low to high, with the pinky, middle, and index fingers, utilizing the pinky to mute string 5.

Full Band

Slow Demo
Gtr. 1   meas. 4,
6–7, 17–18,
22–24

Fig. 12

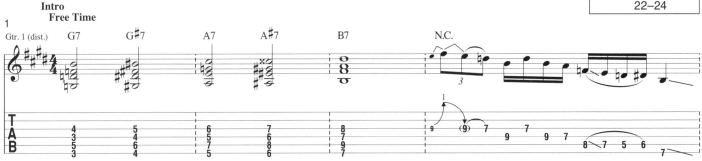

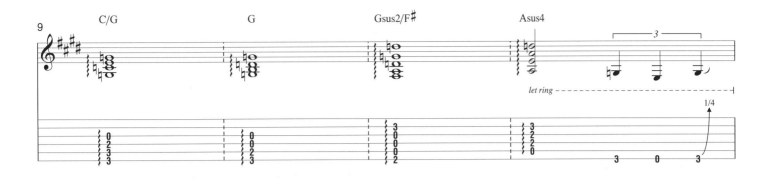

*Chord symbols reflect implied harmony.

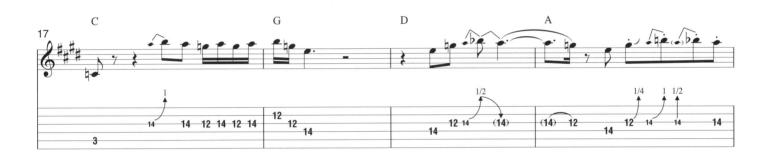

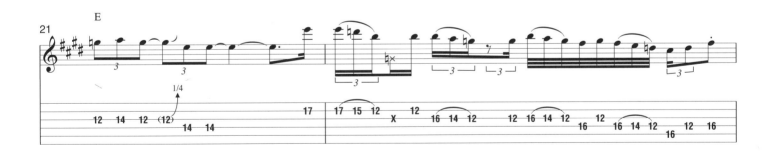

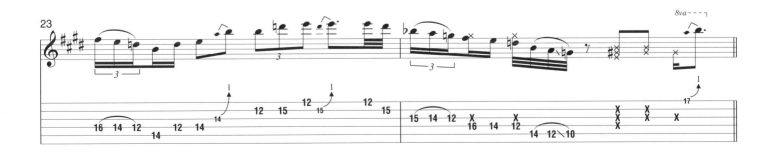

Figure 13—Guitar Solo

After ominously intoning, "…shoot her for me guitar" in vocal verse 2 (not shown), Buchanan teaches a graduate course in blending melody, dramatic note selection, and dynamic phrasing in six eight-measure instrumental verses that build to a stunning crescendo with an explosive firebomb of notes. As he is wont to do, he approaches each verse as new musical terrain to be explored and conquered. Originally copyrighted in 1962 by folk guitarist Billy Roberts, the eight-measure verses of "Hey Joe," with C, G, D, A, and E changes, are theoretically in the key of E and can be analyzed as ♭VI (C), ♭III (G), ♭VII (D), IV (A), and I (E).

Verse 1 (measures 1–8) opens memorably and dramatically, featuring Buchanan with a low volume, clean tone constructing a simple but beautiful, ascending, legato melody with a 3rd (E over C), the root (G), a 5th (A over D), and the 9th and 5th (B and E, respectively, over A) in measures 1–5. Having arrived in the octave positions of the E minor pentatonic scale, he plays a series of repeating bends combined with volume swells to create an emotional "sighing" effect. The sound is actually more important than the specific pitches, though the musical tension generated is released in measure 7, over the I, chord when the one and a half-step bend to the ♭3rd (G) is released to the root (E). In a celestial zone, Buchanan again repeats the one and a half-step bend to the ♭3rd with release back to E across the bar line into measure 9.

Verse 2 (measures 9–16) has Buchanan continuing to execute volume swells, but in conjunction with a circular pattern employing the D, B, A, and G notes from the root-octave position of the E minor pentatonic scale over the ♭VI, ♭III, ♭VII, and IV chords that boosts the momentum forward. A melody reminiscent of a familiar classical theme is produced, and the effect sounds like a clarinet playing staccato lines. He finishes off the verse with bluesy filigree focused on the classic blues notes of the bent A (4th), G (♭3rd), and E (root), as in Fig. 10, for resolution in order to start fresh in the next verse.

Verse 3 (measures 17–24) reveal Buchanan gradually and slyly ramping up the intensity level with increasingly snappy, finely crafted blues licks in measures 17–21 that flow like liquid gold from his fingers. Notice how he descends from the root octave position at the same time to create anticipation, eventually ending up in the root open position in measures 21–23, where he rolls 16th-note figures in a blur of speed. Following a short rest across the bar line to measure 24, Buchanan tips his hand with a dramatic register leap upward to the root octave position, where he cries out a warning with two short shrieks on the ♭7th (D) bent to the root (E).

Verse 4 (measures 25–32) shows Buchanan extending the "cry" with various embellishments through measures 25–28 that increase precipitously in pitch, urgency, and intensity. One of the lessons to be learned is how a repeating riff over changing harmony (chords) makes the riff sound different. Observe that a degree of resolution is attained in measure 28 over the IV (A) chord, with emphasis on the root (A) note that serves to set up measures 29–32 (I chord) as a dynamic prelude to verse 5. Check out how Buchanan relies on one of his favorite Chuck Berry-style repeating unison/harmony bend riffs in the root octave position of the E minor pentatonic scale that evolves into singing 32nd notes that goose the forward momentum with such force as to make it appear that the tempo of the song is accelerating.

Verse 5 (measures 33–40) enters with an avalanche of notes on the ♭VI chord (C) centered around the ♭7th (B♭), major 7th (B), and ♭9th (C♯/D♭) degrees from a combination of scales. Buchanan plays with peak intensity that is highlighted by the jackhammer sequence in measures 34–35 (string 3) that includes the chromatic notes of A, A♯, B, and C over the ♭III (G) and ♭VII (D) chords, which climaxes over the latter with a breathtaking ascending run and a soaring bend from the 5th (A) to the 6th (B). Where a lesser guitarist might just continue to pile on the multi-note extravaganza to the point of numbness, Buchanan intuitively and dynamically slows the onslaught with singing, lyrical blues bends from the root (A) in measure 36, over the IV chord (A). However, he has palpable anger to express in this paean to domestic violence, and in measures 37–40, over the I chord (E), he bashes the root (E) note vehemently on string 2 at fret 17 before returning to the root octave position of the E minor pentatonic scale for headlong, churning patterns similar to measure 33.

Verse 6 (measures 41–48) conclude the landmark solo with another musical rampage that appears to leave his polite Japanese audience stunned. After ramming home the same licks from measure 40 across the bar line into measure 41, over the ♭IV chord (C), Buchanan works hard on string 3 similarly to measure 34, but in descending trajectory and featuring an array of "whistlers" that will dynamically and dramatically end up in the root-open position of the E minor pentatonic scale. With scorching treble raunch and slashing strokes containing a country-blues vibe, he twangs the strings of his sweat-stained Tele to the point of breakage before allowing the tubes in his overheated amp to cool down.

Performance Tip: The licks in measures 33 and 41 should be accessed by barring fret 12 with the index finger. The D note on string 2 and the A♯ note on string 3 should both be played with the pinky in order to make the most efficient transition from the D to the C♯.

Full Band

Slow Demo
Gtr. 1   meas. 20–23,
          30–35, 40–44

Fig. 13

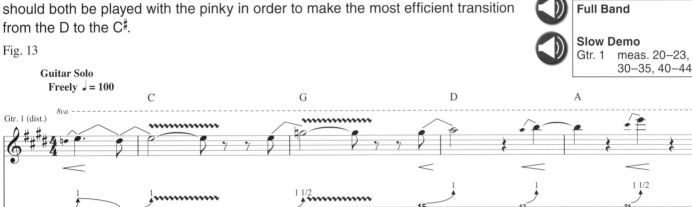

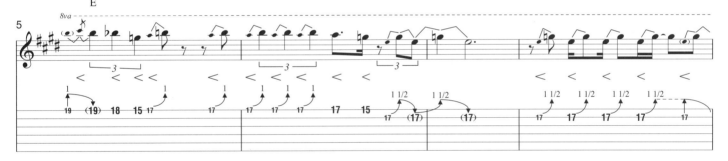

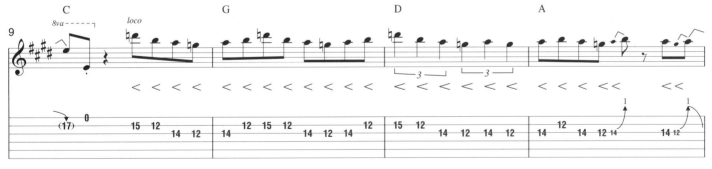

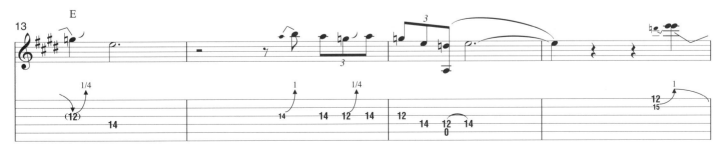

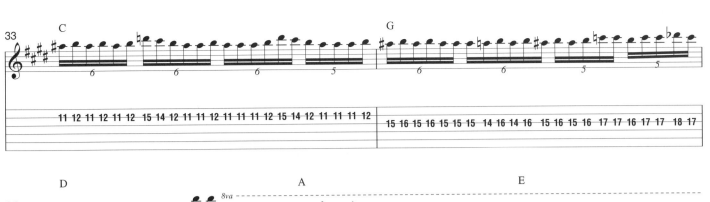

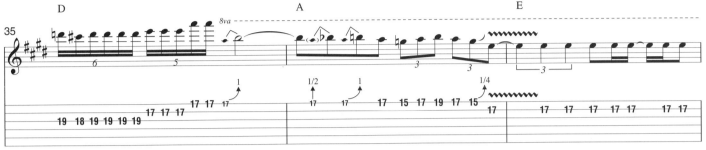

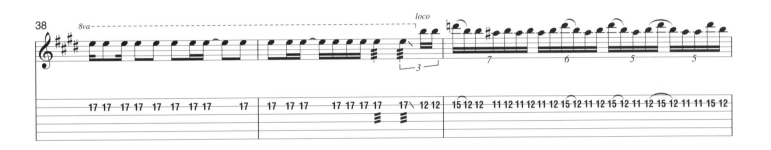

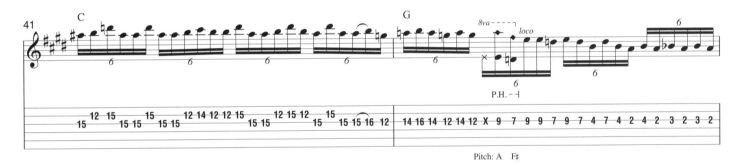

Pitch: A F♯

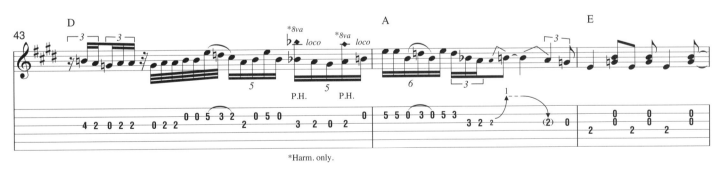

*Harm. only.

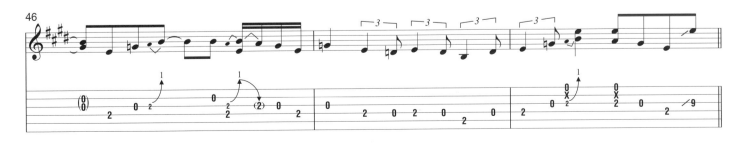

Figure 14—Outro

Buchanan must have been of "sound" mind and body on his Japanese tour if "Hey Joe" is any indication. Giving free rein to his unbridled imagination, he ad libs, improvises, and "free associates" mostly in the E major scale with only unobtrusive organ accompaniment around the E major tonality in the outro. Intelligently, he dials down on his guitar volume, playing on the neck pickup or with the selector switch in the middle position for a rounder, warmer, "bell-like" tone.

As he does in other versions, Buchanan opens his near "soliloquy" with a quote from the American folk song "Oh, Shenandoah" that begins in the last measure of vocal verse 3 (not shown). Extensive use of the major 7th (D#) in the licks that follow take his music out of the blues realm into an area where jazz, pop, and rock meet. In measures 18–21, he "strings" together slippery 4ths and 3rds in a dreamy, pedal steel guitar fantasy that produces musical tension and harkens back to his C&W roots in California.

Silken legato lines from the E major scale on string 3, containing prominent resolution to the root (E), help bridge to measures 24 and 25, where Buchanan again surprises with a logically descending pattern in groupings of three notes. In the former, they consist of notes from the E major scale creatively combined and "palm muted" for a dynamic staccato effect, like raindrops on a tin roof. In the latter, along with measure 26, he eases into the E Mixolydian mode with descending lines on string 1 for a subtle hint of jazzy, melodic blues.

Beginning in measure 27, Buchanan reverses direction and ascends fluidly up through the E major scale until he reaches and trills the root note on string 2 at fret 5 in measure 28 as prelude. What immediately follows are percussive effects created by tapping the strings against the fingerboard with the pick for a musical collage that functions more as abstract sounds rather than specific pitches, as if the song is literally deconstructing. However, just when it seems as if the track has dispersed into the ether, Buchanan brings it back to earth with a series of fluttering trills from the 4th (A) to the major 3rd (G#) that resolves with finality to the sustained root in measure 34.

Performance Tip: In measures 29–32, tap fret 9 on string 2 with the edge of the pick while pulling off from fret 7 to fret 5, and fret 5 to fret 3, respectively, with the ring to index finger.

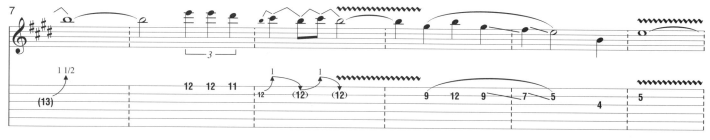

Fig. 14

*Tap first note w/ edge of pick.

**Bounce w/ edge of pick.

HIGH WIRE

(*Hot Wires*, 1987)
Written by Roy Buchanan

Buchanan took an uncharacteristic trip down memory lane with the opening track on his final album. The "bubbly" major chord arpeggios that function as a head and motif throughout the instrumental are reminiscent of melodic patterns that he played on his early 1960s tracks during the golden age of instrumentals. The title is a literal description of the high-register pinch harmonics flying from his strings.

Figure 15—Intro

Rhythm guitarist Donald Kinsey (Gtr. 1) sets the rocking eighth-note groove in measures 1–4 with 3rds, the low open-E string, and related scale notes to define the V (E5) chord. For the next eight measures, he offers bass string riffs relative to the I (A5)–♭III (C5), ♭VII (G)–IV (D), I, I, I–♭III, ♭VII–IV, I, and I changes (Riff A) while Buchanan (Gtr. 2) overlays his lead part. Using extensive "whistling" pinch harmonics (P.H.) in measures 5–6 and 9–10, he creates a "spacey" effect that could have been the "B" side of "Telstar" in 1962. In measures 7–8, 11–12, 15–16, and 19–20, however, he intersperses dynamic improvised licks with selected pinch harmonics from the root position of the A minor pentatonic scale. Though the critical final note in each two-measure improvisation is ostensibly the root (A), the pinch harmonics transform it into the ♭7th (G) for an extra boost forward to the I chord.

In measures 21–36, Buchanan solos with tasty restraint in the E, A, and D composite blues scales to match the V, I, and IV changes that rock on in two-measure increments. Ever the compulsive composer, observe the chromatic lick that follows the root in measures 21, 23, 25, and 27 as a motif for the V and I chords.

Performance Tip: All pinch harmonics (P.H.) should be played with downstrokes.

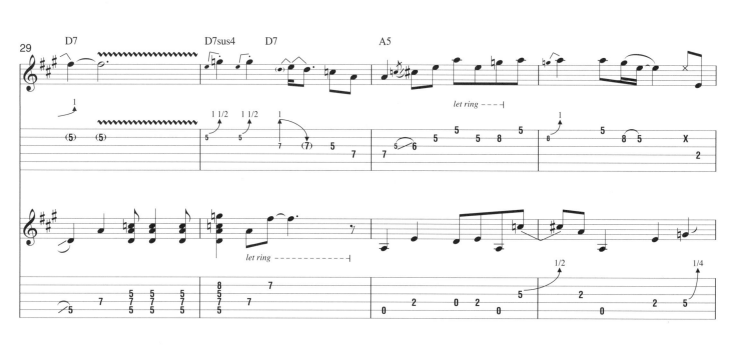

Figure 16—Guitar Solo

With pinch harmonics pinging in all directions like an old fashioned, silver ball pinball machine gone haywire, Buchanan (Gtr. 2) charges into one of his classic improvisational blues-rock grooves in two standard 12-bar choruses with the "slow change." With Kinsey (Gtr. 1) chugging cut boogie patterns and a variety of propulsive dyads underneath like a runaway locomotive, licks tumble from Buchanan's fingers effortlessly as he skillfully combines the A major and A minor pentatonic scales with jubilant abandon.

Among his many musical virtues, Buchanan had few peers when it came to making the transition between the I (A5) and IV (D5) chords. Hence, do not miss measures 4–5 and 16–17 to see and hear the momentum and musical elation generated by his two multi-pitch bends. In the former, the 4th (D) is pumped two steps to the 6th (F♯) on beat 4 of the I chord before sailing across the bar line, where it becomes the tonality-defining major 3rd of D. With delicious, gradual release, one of his many trademarks, Buchanan hits the tangy ♭3rd (F) and the 9th (E) before settling down on the root (D) in preparation for his two-measure residency on the IV chord with repeated pounding on the root. In the latter, he works the concept in reverse by gradually increasing the pitches over the I chord, like a plane taking off, starting on the root (A) and reaching the nasty ♭9th (A♯/B♭), tangy 9th (B), and taut 4th (D) in anticipation of the IV chord.

Check out two other examples of his complete and intelligent command of string bending. In measure 9, over the V (E5) chord, he boosts the ♭5th (B♭) to the 5th (B) in what would ordinarily be a fairly standard move. However, because he is simultaneously pinching harmonics, the note jumps to G (♭3rd) to produce dissonance instead of consonance that is resolved to the root (E) in measure 10. Likewise, notice measure 18, over the IV chord, where he bends the 3rd (F♯) one and a half steps to the 5th (A), thereby nailing down two of the three tones of the D major triad.

Performance Tip: Pinch harmonics ring out the best with a heavy pick held tightly very near the tip and by turning it slightly forward so that the edge of the pick hits the string, as opposed to the flat surface.

Fig. 16

Full Band

Slow Demo
Gtr. 2   meas. 1–4,
        6–16, 17–24

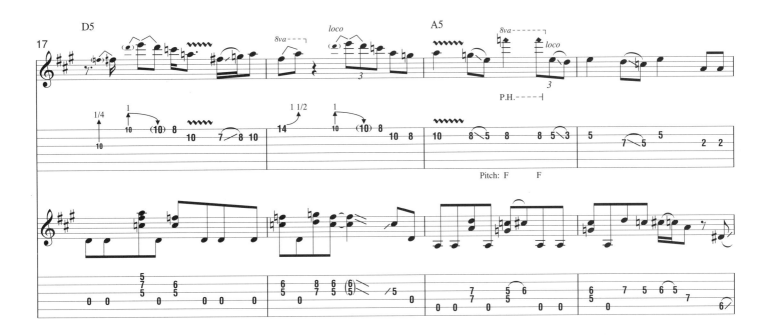

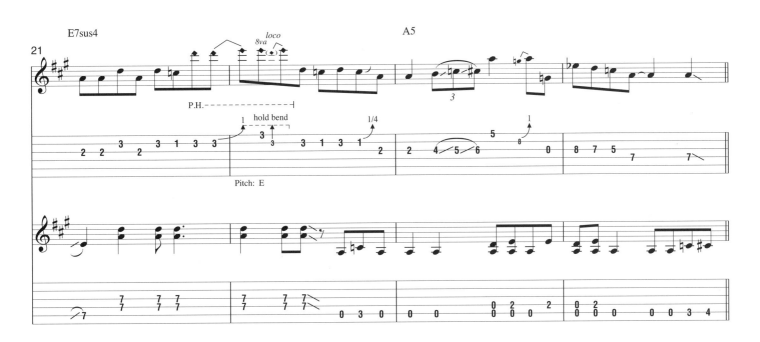

I WON'T TELL YOU NO LIES

(Second Album, 1973)

By Roy Buchanan

Though it is unknown whether they ever met, both Chicago blues legend Son Seals and Roy Buchanan had something in common beyond playing powerful blues from the heart: They both loved playing minor-key progressions. The second of the two heart breaking instrumental minor key blues on his acknowledged best album, "I Won't Tell You No Lies" is another epic outpouring from a man who spoke the truth most eloquently by letting his fingers do the "walking and talking."

Figure 17—Guitar Solo (Measures 1–12)

Following a jazzy piano solo from keyboardist Dick Heintze as a break in the middle of the song, Buchanan (Gtr. 1) picks up where he left off in the A Aeolian mode. Measures 1–12 (Rhy. Fig. 1 by Gtr. 2), comprising a moderately slow blues with the "slow change," function as a de facto "intro" for the second, and final, solo. Relaxed and introspective, Buchanan begins "telling" his musical story with silky bends and legato runs mostly in the root and extension (or "Albert King box") positions, featuring seamless note selection of teasing tension and soothing resolution. Measures 5 and 6, over the iv chord (Dm7), contain especially tasty and lyrical lines consisting of the root (D), ♭7th (C), 6th (B), and 5th (A), in other words, all of the chord tones, save for the ♭3rd (F). Additionally, measures 9 and 10, over the II7 (B7♯11) and the ♭II7–V (B♭7♯11–E) chords, respectively, contain the alternating ♭3rd (D) bent to the 3rd (D♯/E♭) in the former, and the alternating 9th (C) bent to the 3rd (D) in the latter. See that measures 9–11 function as a hip II–V–I sequence.

Performance Tip: Execute all bends in measures 9–10 with the ring finger, backed up by the middle and index.

Fig. 17

Full Band

Slow Demo
Gtr. 1   meas. 5–7

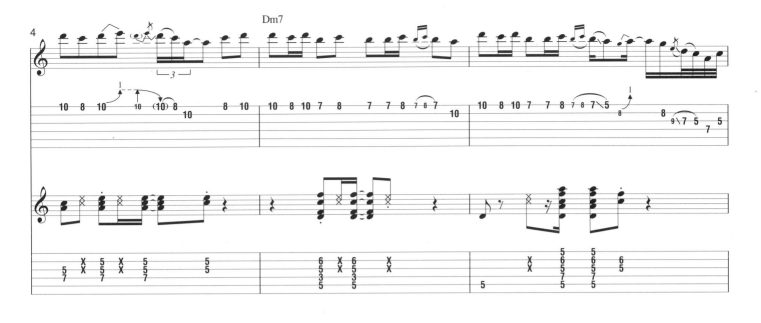

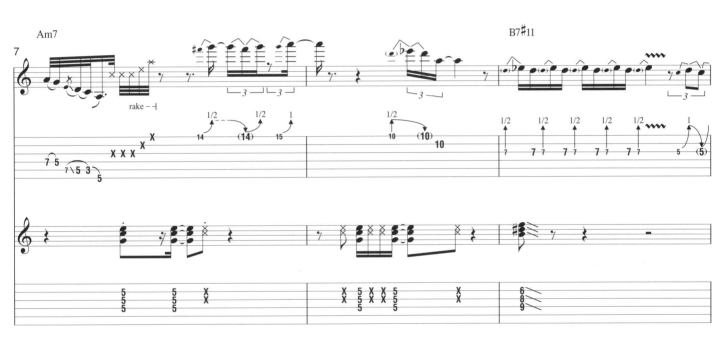

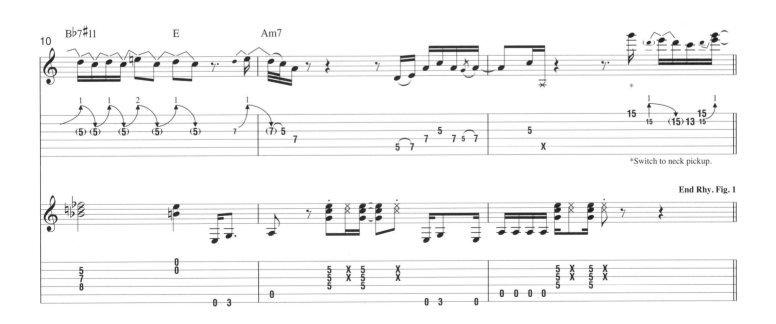

*Switch to neck pickup.

End Rhy. Fig. 1

Figure 18—Guitar Solo (Measures 13–62)

Signaling his intention to enter the next phase of his solo, Buchanan switches to his mellow sounding neck pickup for two 12-bar choruses of legato, melancholy blues with a "country music" accent. In measures 13–24 of the first chorus, he manipulates velvety smooth dyads in 4ths and 3rds, mostly relative to the A Aeolian mode, in order to create gorgeous "glissed" melodies in the manner of steel-guitar players. His thorough understanding of the dyads and their relationship on the fingerboard allows him to navigate the other changes (besides the i), as may be seen in measures 17–18, over the iv change.

Choosing to break away from the dyads in measures 21–22, over the II (B7♯11) and ♭II–V (B♭7♯11–E) chords, Buchanan releases an extraordinary run of fluid, serpentine notes from the A Aeolian mode that pour out like water splashing on stones in a mountain brook while incurring anticipation. Resolution to the root (A) occurs in measure 23, over the i (Am7), following a hip lick of the 9th (B), ♭7th (G), and 4th (D) that simultaneously hints at the harmony while adding a dash of musical tension.

In measures 25–36 of the third chorus, Buchanan takes advantage of the laid back groove, along with the direction his solo has taken, and pushes the envelope into the realm of jazz. With an approach that would have benefited from his big Gibson L-5 in the 1950s and further cements the connection to Wes Montgomery, he solos with octaves from start to finish, creating bittersweet melodies that stick in the memory. Clearly he spent a substantial amount of time soaking up the form and content of jazz guitar, and he composes a beautifully realized arrangement derived from the A Aeolian mode. Starting with a "hooky," repeating one-measure motif containing the root (A), 4th (D), and ♭3rd (C) notes combined with the 5th (E) and ♭7th (G) in measures 25–27, over the i change, he next articulates the iv chord in measures 29–30 with the root (D), 2nd (E), 4th (G), 5th (A), 6th (B), and ♭7th (C) notes. In previous choruses, Buchanan had opted to play against the changes and let the potent, dissonant effect of the 7♯11 chords in measures 9 and 10 of the 12-bar progression provide the tension. However, in measures 33 (B7♯11) and 34 (B♭7♯11), he leans on the ♯11 notes (F and E, respectively) to intensify the natural edginess of the voicings, while complementing the V chord (E) with a double-octave 5th (B). However, he does not slow the momentum by hitting the root (E) before resolving to the root (A) in measure 35, over the i chord, with another double octave.

Measures 37–48 dramatically shift with a flick of his selector switch to the cutting bridge pickup. With a far more aggressive attack, Buchanan dynamically evolves to the climactic 12-bar chorus in terms of intensity with cutting A minor pentatonic licks virtually all above the octave. Dig how he erupts with anguished cries wrenched out of his axe with the most pugnacious blues phrasing this side of Jimmy Nolen or Buddy Guy, while pushing his strings to the limits of their tensile strength. His sense of composition, pacing, and timing were never better than in this one chorus, which a lesser guitarist would consider their crowning career achievement. In measures 37–38, over the i chord, he repeatedly pops the root (A) by bending from the ♭7th (G) to create tension where static resolution would normally occur.

In measure 39, however, he emphasizes the ♭7th dead on combined with the 5th (E), by bending up from the 4th (D), for a squealing slap in the ear guaranteed to get attention in an auspicious entrance. Beginning on beat 3 of measure 40, over the i change, and continuing through measure 41, over the iv chord (Dm7), Buchanan adds contrast and dynamics by rapidly picking notes in the 12th position of the A minor pentatonic scale with emphasis on the root (D) and 5th (A) notes combined with percussive mutes, resulting in an extra boost of forward motion. In measure 42, over the iv chord, he takes a classic blues lick consisting of the 4th (D) bent to the 5th (E), followed by the 5th, root (A), ♭7th (G), and 5th in the root-octave position of the A minor pentatonic scale, and plays it so fast as to transform it into another blast of ringing treble that relates back to measure 39. He ups the tension quotient with a rush by way of a wailing bend of the major 7th (C♯) one and a half steps to the 9th (E) that crosses the bar line to the i chord, where it functions as the 5th. Capping the peak intensity, he adds furiously fast vibrato on the bent 5th to produce his famous "horse whinny," followed by a dynamic, dramatic rest. Resolution is reached in measure 44 of the i chord with the root (A) note picked straight on and by the ♭7th bent one step.

Buchanan "trots out" a new idea for the II (B7♯11) and ♭II–V (B♭7♯11–E) changes in measures 45 and 46, respectively. In the former, he uses voice-like volume swells of the ♭7th (A) bent to the root (B), along with the bent root and ♭7th alternated in a "crying" manner. In the latter, he bends the major 7th (A) one and a half steps to the 9th (C) twice for prickly tension before resolving to the V chord with the ♭7th (D) bent to the root (E). In a sensational sequence, even for him, Buchanan brings this segment of his solo to a proper close by quickly bending the ♭3rd (G) one step, which resolves across the bar line to the i (Am7) in measure 47. Not finished yet with his stunningly creative melancholy expression, he bends the ♭7th (G) a half step to the major 7th (G♯/A♭) and picks the ♭7th, emphasized by the 6th (F♯) bent a half step two times to the ♭7th, to keep up the momentum in the penultimate measure of the chorus. When he finally reaches his destination in measure 48, he reverts back to the A Aeolian mode for a striking, descending melodic line containing the added 6th (F♯) from the Dorian mode, along with the ♭6th (F), 5th (E), ♭3rd (C), root (A), and ♭7th, which encourages anticipation to the last 12-bar chorus.

Measures 49-62 represent a cooling down of the inflamed passions that preceded them. Buchanan returns to the root position of the A minor pentatonic scale from whence he began in the intro to his solo. Amazingly, he drops right back into a legato flow of seemingly unlimited improvisational ideas that simultaneously follow the chord changes with subtlety and nuance. This can be clearly seen in measures 53–54, over the iv chord (Dm7), where the ♭7th (C) and 5th (A) complement the tonality in the former, and the 9th (E) and 4th (G) notes tweak the tension in the latter on the way to solid resolution in measures 55–56, over the i chord (Am7), via emphasis on the root (A).

In measure 57, over the II chord (B7♯11), he once again goes to the ♭7th (A) to concurrently define the dominant tonality and to "lead" to measure 58, where he unfurls a stunner. A long string of notes, derived from the root position of the A minor pentatonic scale and similar in intent to measures 21–22, float down over the ♭II (B♭7♯11) chord in pairs while producing refined anticipation due to the notes, as well as musical gravity that ends on the 4th (A) of the V chord (E). Without a pause, Buchanan just as gracefully reverses direction while accelerating and resolving with deliberateness to the root (E), bent up from the ♭7th (D). Still not satisfied that he has had his full say on the "subject" of his minor key musical dissertation, in measure 59, over the i chord, he rips into his G string at fret 9, bending two and a half glorious steps from the 5th (E) to the root (A) and gradually releases it. Buchanan completes his blues master thesis with the classic blues lick of the 4th (D) bent to the 5th (E), released and pulled off to the ♭3rd (C) with resolution to the root (A), which he repeats in measure 60, the last measure of the last 12-bar chorus. However, even though the band has ceased playing, Buchanan feels compelled to stretch unaccompanied for two more measures. He sustains the root in measure 61, followed by a pull-off from the 5th to ♭5th, which he then sustains across the bar line into measure 62, lending an air of unresolved tension perfectly in keeping with his complex and contradictory personality.

Performance Tip: The octaves in measures 25–36 should be accessed as such:
On strings 6 and 4 and 5 and 3, use the index and ring fingers. On strings 4 and 2
and 3 and 1, use the index and pinky fingers.

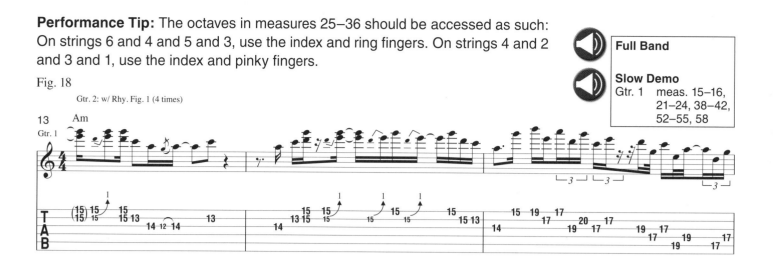

Full Band

Slow Demo
Gtr. 1   meas. 15–16,
21–24, 38–42,
52–55, 58

Fig. 18

Gtr. 2: w/ Rhy. Fig. 1 (4 times)

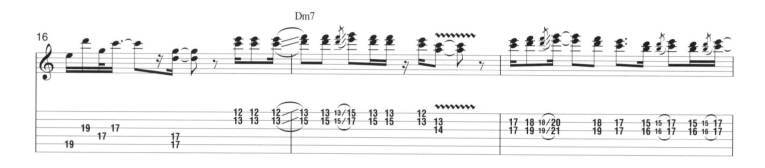

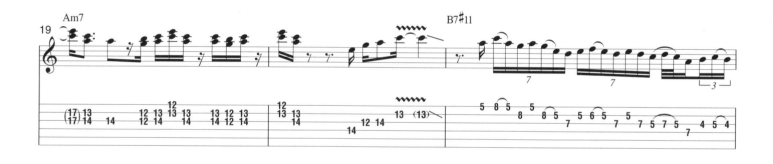

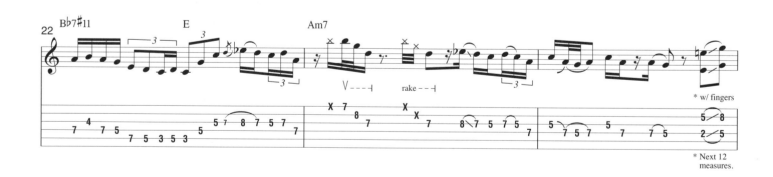

* w/ fingers

* Next 12
measures.

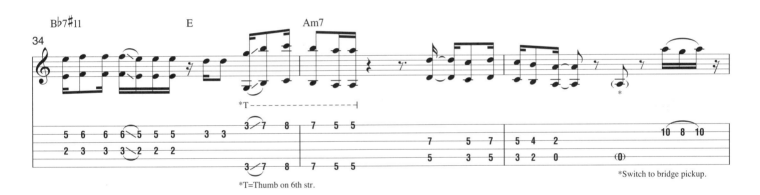

*T=Thumb on 6th str.

*Switch to bridge pickup.

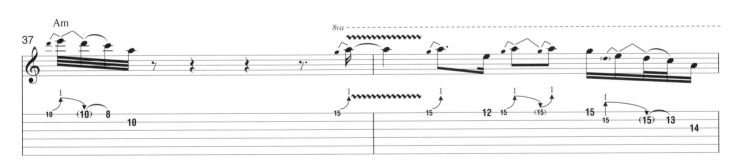

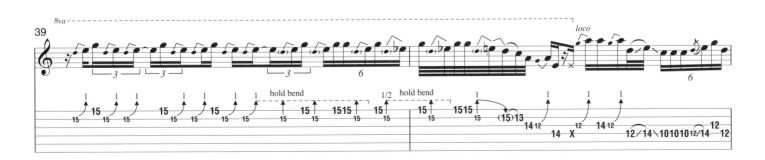

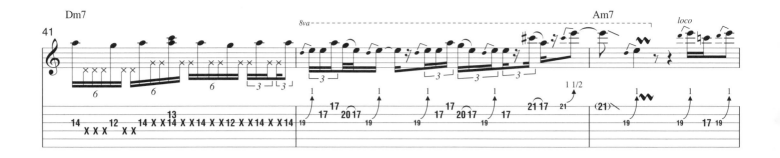

*Vol. swells.

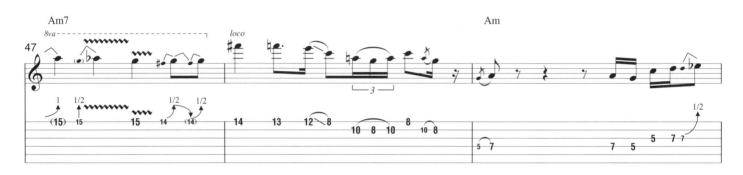

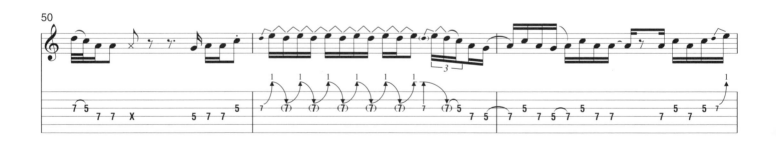

I WON'T TELL YOU NO LIES

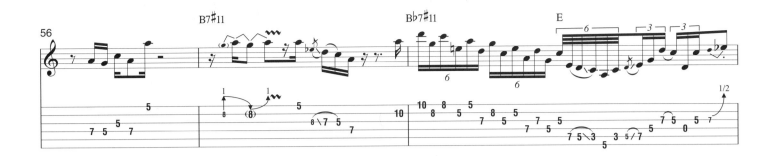

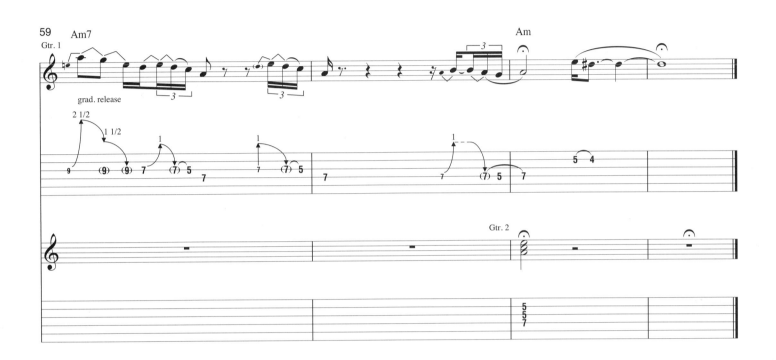

THE MESSIAH WILL COME AGAIN

(*Roy Buchanan*, 1972)
Written by Roy Buchanan

The best parts of the pseudo-psychedelic single "Black Autumn," from *The Prophet* (1970), released in 2004 with additional tracks, are the two instrumental breaks contributed by Buchanan that contain the future chord changes and melody of "The Messiah Will Come Again." His religious beliefs are unknown, but his haunting melody is unquestionably spiritual, and the song remains one of his signature compositions.

Figure 19—Intro (Section A)

The 12-measure intro consists of three four-measure chord sequences played with appropriately "churchy" organ pads. Measures 1–8 descend twice with Asus4–Am, Cmaj13–Cmaj7–Dm/C–C, Dm(add9)–Dm–Dm7, and Esus4–E7 changes. Measures 9–12 are altered to: Am(add9)–Am–Am(add9)–Am, G6–G, F6–Fmaj7–G/F–F, and Bsus4–B–B7. Over the briskly moving harmony, Buchanan (Gtr. 1) effectively restricts his activity to the A minor pentatonic scale in the 12th position to produce a musical statement of timeless melodies.

Though delicate in tone and phrasing, the sweet improvisation shows intelligent note selection relative to the harmony. Buchanan simply and eloquently resolves to the root (A) and 5th (A) in measures 1 and 3, respectively, while ending on the 5th (E) in measure 4. In measures 5–8, he bends the ♭7th (G) to the root (A) in measure 5, over the i chord (Am), and emphasizes the 5th (C) and 3rd (A) in measure 7, over the VI (F) change. Observe that Buchanan creates tension in measure 8, over the V chord (E), but resolves it with the repeated root (A), along with the vibratoed ♭3rd (C), in measure 9 (i chord).

Performance Tip: In measure 10, bend the 5th (D) on string 2 at fret 15 with the ring finger, backed up by the middle and index, while accessing the root (G) on string 1 at fret 15 with the pinky.

Full Band

Slow Demo
Gtr. 1   meas. 7–10

Fig. 19

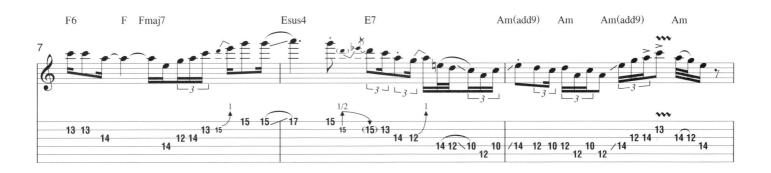

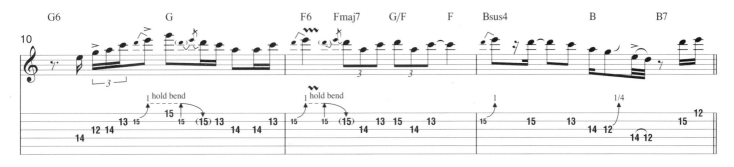

Figure 20—Section C

Starting with an unaccompanied pickup from the last measure of the recitation (Section B, not shown), Buchanan (Gtr. 1) lets loose his most pleading, melodic "head," courtesy of the "round" sound of the Tele neck pickup. The chord progression has now evolved to a streamlined i (Am)–VII (G)–VI (F)–II (B)–V (E) progression derived from Flamenco music and similar to other classic rock such as "Walk Don't Run" (in A major), "I'll Be Back" (Beatles), "All Along the Watchtower," the solo in "Stairway to Heaven," and "Sultans of Swing" (in D minor). However, the II chord is the kicker that changes the whole effect of the progression and the melody, and may be seen as part of the II–V–i progression favored greatly by jazz musicians due to its characteristic forward momentum.

Through the most minimal of means, Buchanan fashions perhaps his most personal expression of the anguish emanating from the depths of his soul. Naturally, his exceptionally fluid phrasing, powered by his unmatched command of string manipulation, is and always was the ultimate source of his legendary artistry. But, in addition, be aware of his choices of the critical "target note" over each chord: Am = ♭3rd (C), G = 3rd (B), F = 3rd (A), B = 3rd (D♯), and E = root (E). As should be seen and understood, he emphasizes the tonality-defining 3rd, both major and minor, save for the V chord (E), where he seeks and finds solid resolution to the root note. Proving his virtually infallible intuition, he bends the D♯ (from the II chord) a half step to the root (E) of the V chord in a dynamic, dramatic, uplifting move.

Performance Tip: All bends may be executed with the ring finger, backed by the middle and index.

Fig. 20

THE MESSIAH WILL COME AGAIN

Figure 21—Guitar Solo (Section E)

Buchanan takes on the challenge of improvising three eight-measure verses to explore the melodic possibilities inherent in the contemplative harmony. In measures 1–8, he espouses the value of economy as he releases a primal scream on the bridge pickup by working the D note on string 2 at fret 15 for all it is worth through seven measures. Make no mistake, the choice of note was not capricious. Bent one and then one and a half steps over the Am, it becomes the 5th (E) and the ♭6th (F) from the A Aeolian mode, respectively, creating degrees of tension. Bent one step over the G, it becomes the harmonious 6th (E) from the G major scale. Bent one step over the F, it functions as the sweet major 7th (E), bent a half step as the bluesy ♭7th (E♭), and then as the 6th (D) when released. Then it gets even more interesting in measures 5–6, over the B chord, where Buchanan seesaws back and forth between the D (♭3rd), and D♯ (3rd) alternating dissonance and consonance. In measure 7 over the E change, he merely bends one step to reach the root (E) for the expected and welcome resolution at this juncture of the progression. However, measure 8, with the rhythm section dynamically resting, consists of a blistering, dramatic, chromatic-laced ascending run up string 1 (E), with the string clanging open and interspersed throughout.

Continuing straight into Am at the top of the next chorus (measures 9–16) without stopping, Buchanan keeps picking right past the end of the fingerboard. In measures 10 (G) and 11 (F), he just keeps dramatically ascending higher and higher over the pick guard, out near the bridge. While basically shifting to chromatic notes, with some exceptions, he reaches the note E in the sonic neighborhood where only dogs can hear, before reversing direction down to beat 1 of measure 12 (F). Though analyzing the pitches is instructive from a theoretical point of view, be aware that they are not perceived distinctly as such, and it is the dynamic, scratchy, percussive effect and the rapidity with which they are played that adds a startling, climactic, tension-filled element to the second instrumental verse.

Just as dramatically, Buchanan re-enters the world of actual fretted notes on beat 2 of measure 12 (F), highlighted by arcing bends of D (6th) to E (major 7th) that create a solid and welcome dose of major, diatonic tonality to bring the solo back down to earth. In keeping with his overall intent, the slippery bends produce an imploring and beseeching, deeply expressive sound likewise experienced in measures 13–14, over the B change, even as emphasis on the root note (B) confirms tonality. Again revealing his musical smarts, as well as expressiveness and technique, Buchanan continues bending the A to B bend into measure 15, over the E chord, to produce a degree of anticipation before resolving to the root (E) in measure 16.

Measures 17–24, the third and final solo verse, open with what has been a motif throughout the song, as Buchanan bends the D on string 2 at fret 15 to make it "cry" in sorrow in yet another, different climax. Over the Am, G, and F changes, he plays alternating one and half-step bends with the critical release, gradually accelerating the momentum in measure 20 (F) to exponentially increase the tension factor. Again in this instance, the striking emotional effect is more important than the actual pitches as an extremely powerful improvisational tool, though it is worth "noting" that, due to pinch harmonics, the pitches in measure 20 are in reality B (♯11) rather than E (major 7th) in the one-step bends. Measures 22–22, over B and E, respectively, are virtually identical to measures 14 and 15. Signaling the impending return to the "head" in Section F (not shown), the concluding section of the song, Buchanan switches back to the velvety piccolo-sounding neck pickup and offers a "pickup" lick relative to the one that precedes measure 1 of Section C.

Performance Tip: When playing past the end of the fingerboard, as in measures 9–12, lightly rest the index finger on string 1 as if playing "false" harmonics.

Full Band

Slow Demo
Gtr. 1   meas. 8–11, 20

Fig. 21

*Muted notes continue moving up past fretboard.
Approximate pitches are indicated in notation.

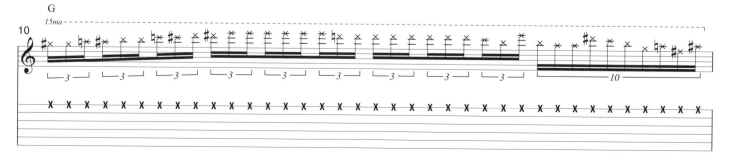

PETE'S BLUES

(*Roy Buchanan*, 1972)
By Roy Buchanan

The reference in the title may be to Pete's Tavern, the oldest continually operating bar room and restaurant in New York City from 1864 that was a famous hangout for O. Henry. It also was a favorite watering hole for Buchanan, and he is pictured sitting there at a table with "Nancy" and a brew on the cover of *Loading Zone* (a pun?).

Figure 22—Measures 1–44

A modal blues masterpiece that introduced the genius of Roy Buchanan to the guitar world, it is virtually one long solo 7:15 in length in the "people's key" of C major (perhaps to give keyboardist Dick Heintze a fingering break on the long, repetitive ride). Measures 1–44 comprise a musical journey that roams from Chicago to the Middle East and beyond. As was often his "modus operandi," Buchanan combines various related scales, including the C minor blues scale, C Mixolydian mode, and the ultra-cool C bebop 7th scale with the hip major 7th degree. In measures 1–24, he squeezes "Nancy" with burning passion, creating long, sustained, blues-fueled lines laced with twisting bends. But when he gets to beat 3 of measure 24, he becomes a "snake charmer," playing astonishing "desert melodies" with the major 7th (B), root (C), ♭6th (A♭), and ♭9th (D♭) notes. Literally in another musical "world," he maintains the exotic ambience all the way to measure 44. He incorporates repeating slithery bends from the 3rd (E) to the 4th (F) on string 2 at fret 5 in measure 28 and the 4th (F) to the 5th (G) in measure 31. On string 3 at fret 5, in measure 29, he executes pinch harmonics on the root to produce the 5th (G), along with bending it to the ♭6th (A♭) and the major 7th (B).

Performance Tip: Combine Gtrs. 1 and 2 in measures 1–3.

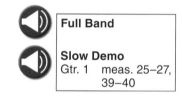

Full Band

Slow Demo
Gtr. 1   meas. 25–27, 39–40

Fig. 22

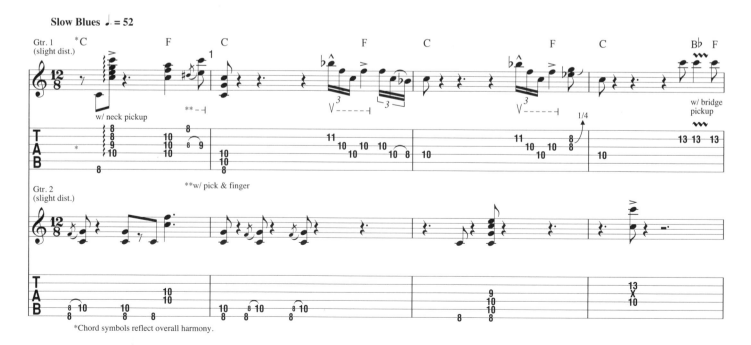

*Notes sounded unintentionally by vibrato on string 2.

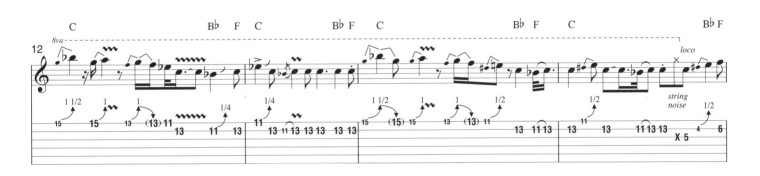

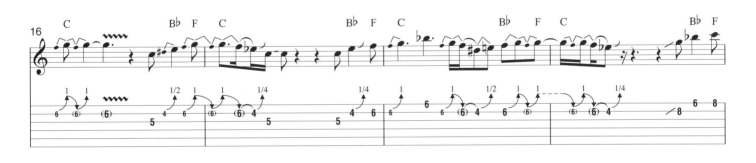

Pitch: E F E

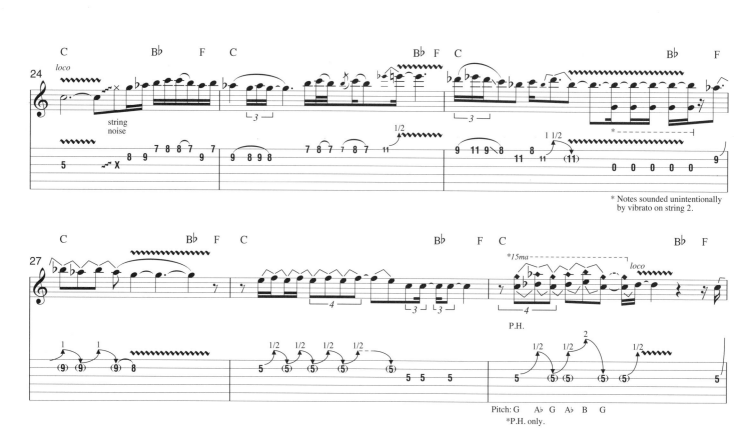

* Notes sounded unintentionally
by vibrato on string 2.

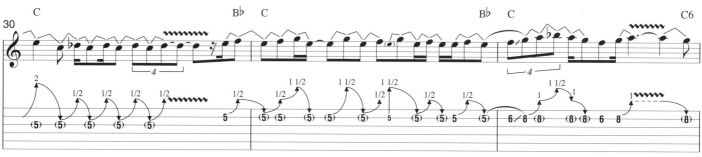

Pitch: G   Ab   G   Ab   B   G
*P.H. only.

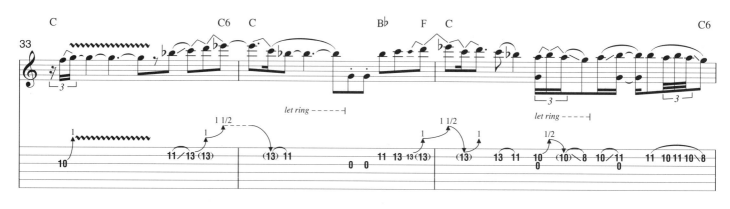

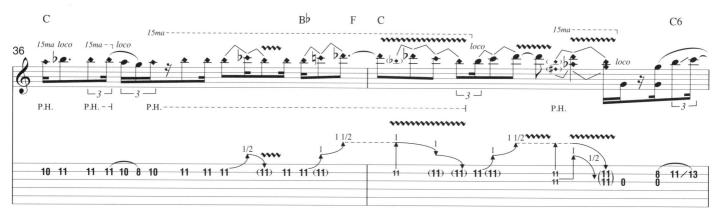

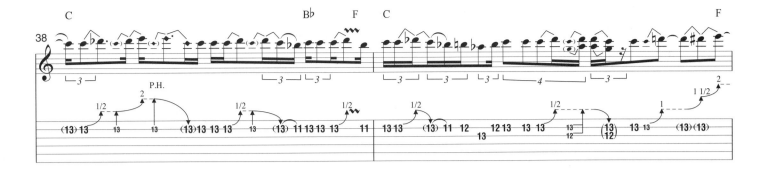

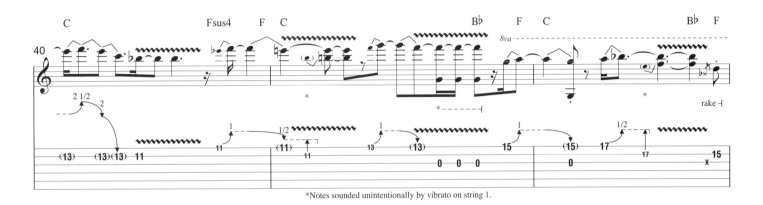

*Notes sounded unintentionally by vibrato on string 1.

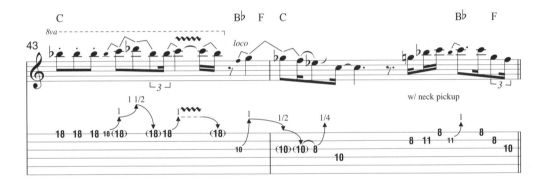

Figure 23—Measures 62–88

Flaunting his unfettered imagination and intense concentration, Buchanan (Gtr. 1) solos on with wild abandon. In this section, he builds quickly to a tremendous head of steam before pulling one of his many patented, dynamic moves out of his bag of "tricks." Measure 62 begins modestly enough with the root (C) sustained and vibratoed, followed in measure 63 by a dramatic series of bends from the ♭3rd (E♭) at fret 11 on string 1 of a half step to the 3rd (E), one step to the 4th (F), and two hefty steps to the 5th (G). Buchanan then dials back the tension in measure 64 by reversing the sequence of bends until he works his way to the root position of the C minor pentatonic scale and continues descending all the way down to resolution on the root (C) on string 6. His well thought out composition is revealed in measure 65, where he turns up the heat with a lightning fast run up the scale, culminating in a wickedly dynamic triple-stop lick of C/G/E♭ (root/5th/♭3rd) as his fingers scamper up the strings in a headlong forward run. Ripped repeatedly in a blur of raked notes, the implied first inversion Cm triad contributes blues grit in dynamic contrast to the descending "hot country guitar" licks, with open strings à la James Burton in measure 66 ending on resolution to the root.

In measure 67, Buchanan utilizes a brilliant succession of palm muted, dramatic, ascending triple-stops related to the C major triad on strings 4, 3, and 2 to produce riveting anticipation. He continues unabated through measures 68–69 as he climbs up string 2 with the C Mixolydian mode in his famous "stuttering" manner that produces hair-raising musical tension. He peaks on the major tonality 3rd (E) on string 1 via a half-step bend from the E♭ (♭3rd) before building extensive, tightly-coiled licks on string 3 in the root position of the C minor pentatonic scale, producing jaw-dropping tension in measures 70–74. Observe how it is exacerbated by bending the living hell out of string 3 with dizzying pitch variations, even as he resolves it in measures 69–70 and 72–73 by nailing the I (C9) and IV (Fsus4 and F) changes with their respective root notes. However, in measures 74–75, Buchanan cranks it back up with searing pinch harmonics joined to punishing bends for a series of notes that fly from his guitar like a pack of wildcats descending on their prey. Reining in his wildest impulses, he plays reverse multi-pitch bends with rippling vibrato in measures 76–77 in the root and extension positions of the C minor pentatonic scale that wail and moan like wounded beasts.

In measures 78–88 Buchanan drops a "bass bomb," in a display of spectacular technique unexpected even from him, after having descended down to the first position of the C bebop 7th scale and ending on the open sixth string (E). With his unerring ear for pitch and utilizing the tuning peg—hey, no whammy bar for him!—he dramatically detunes his lowest bass string down to G and then C in measures 78–79. (Note: In measure 78, the harmony changes to just C9, with a quick grace D♭9 for the duration of an eighth note used as a "pump" chord.) Beginning in measure 80 and through to measure 83, he plays short, gruff, bass register blues licks on strings 6 and 5 in the C composite blues scale, with the lowered C on string 6 rumbling like distant thunder. In measure 84, he opts to rise up from the depths with a dramatic line of ascending notes derived from the C major scale that alternate with the open sixth string as the octave C is reached at fret 15, where he commences to reverse direction. By measure 86, he has completed another dynamic circuit and is back to the open sixth string, while in measure 87, he detunes even lower, down to B♭, before beginning to gear back up to C in measure 89 (not shown) to take the song over and out.

Performance Tip: Well-lubricated tuning machines in excellent working order are required in order to detune smoothly à la "Roy." In addition, the string must have been installed on the post with enough wraps to prevent slippage or literally coming off, especially when bringing it back up to pitch.

Full Band

Slow Demo
Gtr. 1   meas. 66–68,
              75, 85

Fig. 23

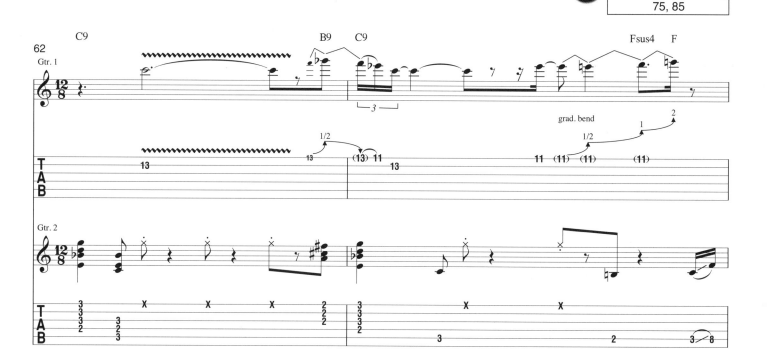

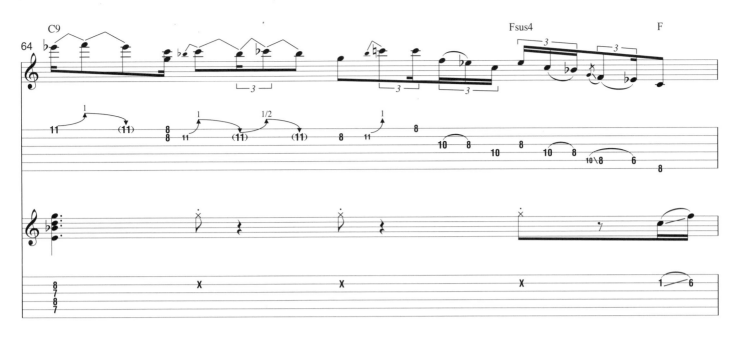

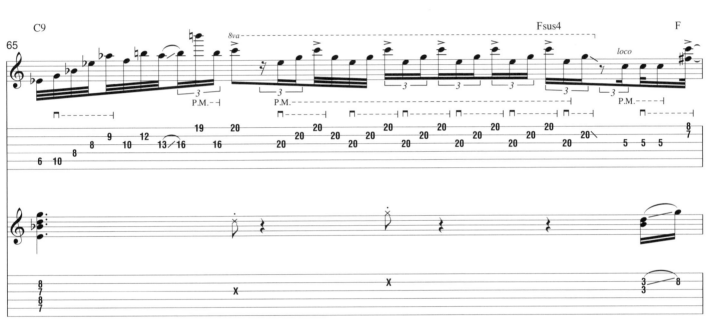

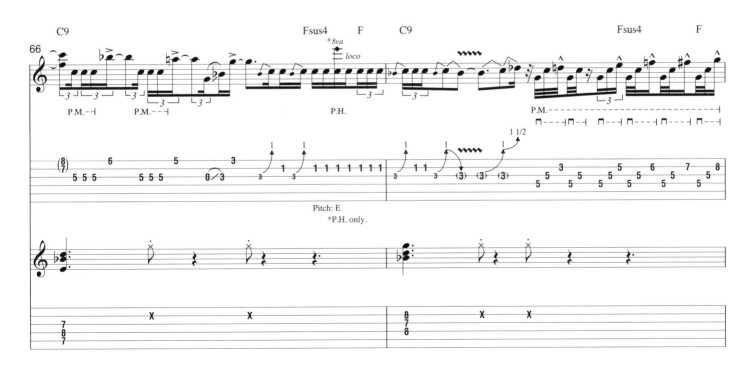

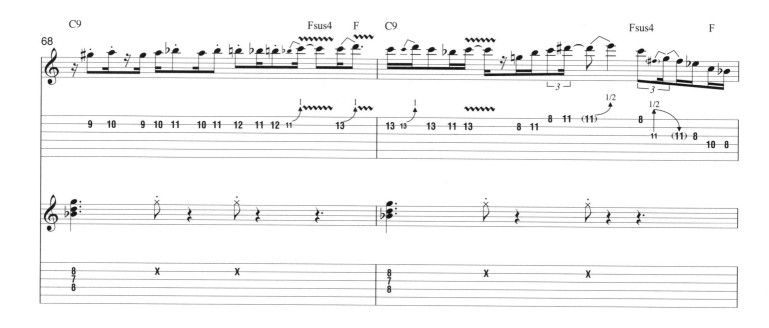

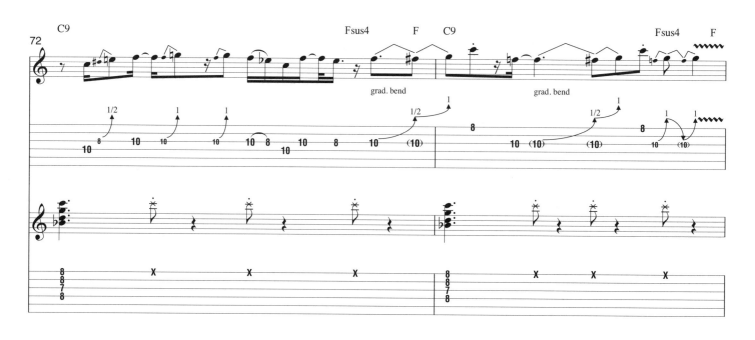

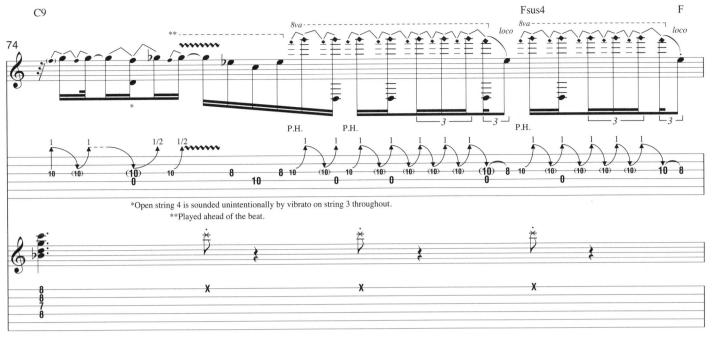

*Open string 4 is sounded unintentionally by vibrato on string 3 throughout.
**Played ahead of the beat.

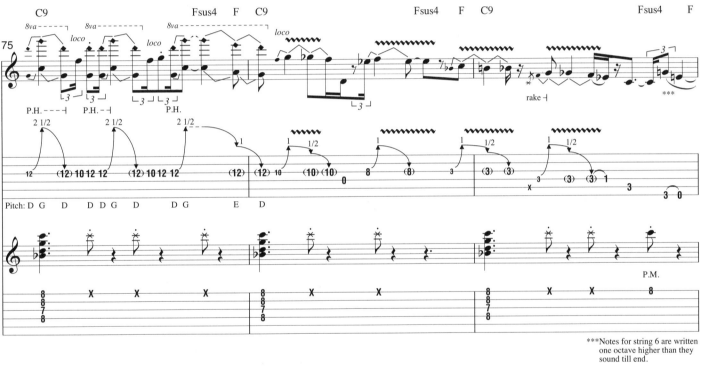

***Notes for string 6 are written
one octave higher than they
sound till end.

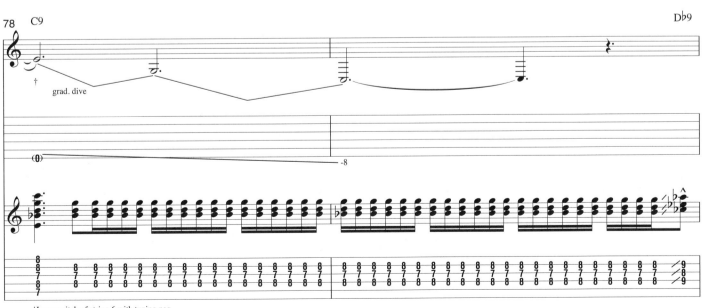

†Lower pitch of string 6 with tuning peg.

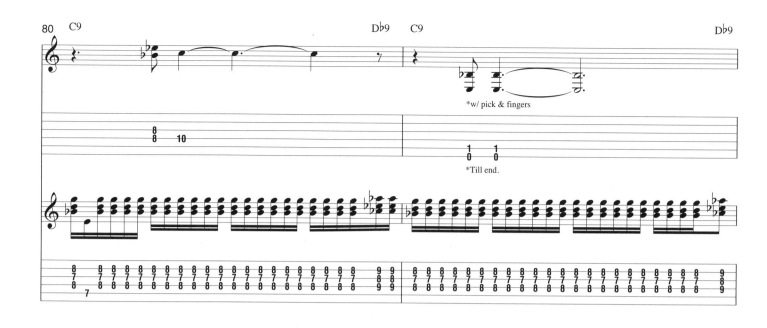

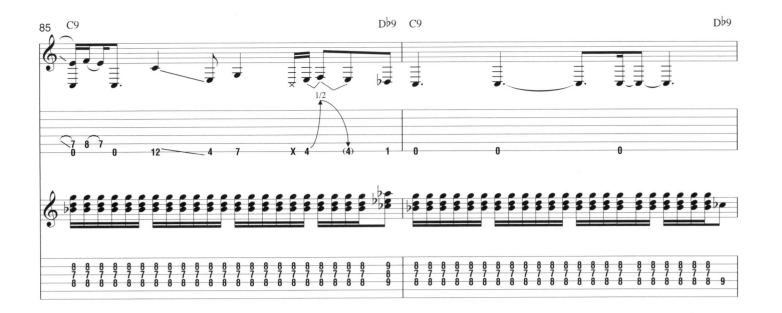

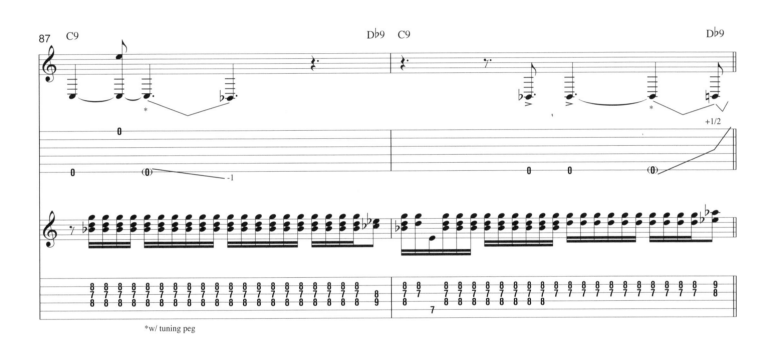

*w/ tuning peg

PETER GUNN
(*Dancing on the Edge*, 1986)
Theme Song from the Television Series
By Henry Mancini

Few younger guitar fans are aware of Duane Eddy's thumping 1960 version of "Peter Gunn," let alone the original from 1958. The latter was the jazzed-up blues theme song to the TV detective show of the same name that ran from 1958–61. It garnered two Grammys and an Emmy award for composer Henry Mancini and features future composer/conductor John Williams playing the signature riff on piano. Freddie King quoted it within the context of a 12-bar progression in his classic "Hide Away" in 1961, and, in 1986, Eddy collaborated with the Art of Noise for a "Twang Mix" version. Buchanan immediately created his own bold statement on his second Alligator album when he made the I-chord vamp the heavyweight opening track that punches like Mike Tyson.

Figure 24—Section A

The "head" contains three sections: A, B, and C. Section A shows one of the most famous and classic bass lines ever recorded. Even today, it is often one of the first riffs beginning guitarists and bassists learn due to its simplicity and irresistible bluesy appeal. Originally in the key of F, no doubt to accommodate the horn players, Buchanan wisely placed his ferocious version in the guitar-friendly key of E. Played exclusively on string 6 with the root (E) as the open sixth string, and the 2nd (F♯), ♭3rd (G), and 4th (A) notes from the E Aeolian mode, it is a timeless loop that may be recycled endlessly and hypnotically. Check out the way Buchanan (Gtr. 1) adds subtle quarter-step bends to the 2nd and ♭3rd notes for that cool blues touch that he could never resist, whatever the song selection.

Performance Tip: Utilize the index, middle, and pinky fingers, in sequence, to access the fretted notes.

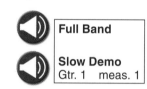

Fig. 24

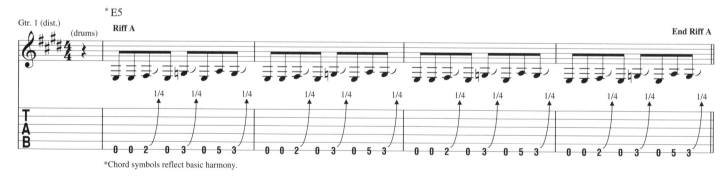

*Chord symbols reflect basic harmony.

Figure 25—Section B

Section B is a guitar version of the original horn section line as interpreted and embellished by Buchanan (Gtr. 2). The 16 measures consists of two similar eight-measure progressions with the ubiquitous E5 harmony and a memorable, bluesy melody created by the ♭7th (D), 5th (B), and hip ♭9th (F) in measures 1–4. However, where the original line in measures 5–9 emphasized the ear-tweaking ♭9th and resolved from the ♭3rd to the major 3rd, Buchanan turns it into a lightning-fast, high energy blues-rocking riff emphasizing the less jazzy ♭7th (D) and 5th (B) notes. Observe his use of the open first string (E) in conjunction with the 6th (C♯) bent a half step to the ♭7th in measure 1, makes a nasty, abrasive sound in keeping with the general electric mayhem of the track.

Performance Tip: In measures 5–6, utilize the index, ring, and pinky fingers for the B, C♯, and D notes on string 2. The index and ring fingers should be used for the Tommy gun hammers and pulls in the first and second endings.

Fig. 25

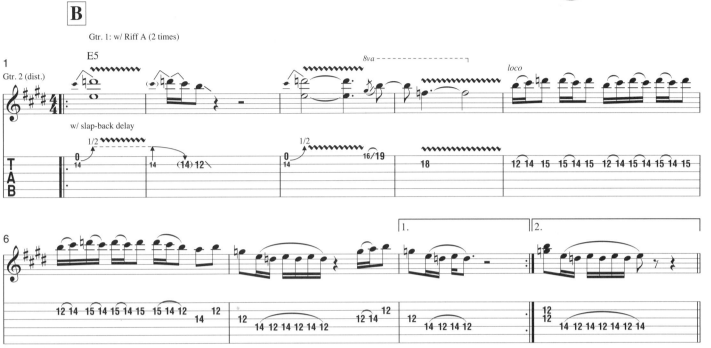

Figure 26—Section C

The aggressive stop-time licks in measures 1–4 are based on the dynamic sequence in the Duane Eddy classic played by tenor saxist Steve Douglas, but do not appear on the original Henry Mancini version. However, where Douglas ended his three licks on the root, ♭7th, and root, Buchanan emphasizes the 5th (B), ♭7th (D), and root (E), along with slipping in a blues approved, bent-string lick of the 4th (A) to the 5th in measure 4 on the way to the root for resolution. In addition, where the Eddy arrangement changes harmony (I–IV–I), Buchanan deigns to remain on the I chord (E) in keeping with his presumed desire to maintain maximum thrust in the composition. Note that he repeats the stop-time after the guitar solo as a dynamic compositional device.

Performance Tip: Anchor the index finger on strings 2 and 1 at fret 12.

Fig. 26

Figure 27—Guitar Solo

If the "Peter Gunn" guitar solo was a rocket flight, it would mimic astronaut Alan B. Shepard going up in his Mercury capsule in 1961 as the first American in space: a powerful lift-off that picks up tremendous speed and altitude, followed by a downward trajectory and a smooth landing. The first stage of Buchanan's ascent takes place in measures 1–12, where he arcs away from his "launching pad" in the root, extension, and upper reaches of the E minor pentatonic scale with exceptionally long, sustained notes. Check out how he manufactures high-torque tension by avoiding the root (E) note for resolution until measures 6–7, instead bending to the 5th (B), ♭7th (D), and ♭5th (B♭) notes via one, one and a half, and even two and a half steps, as seen in measure 11.

Breaking the bonds of earth, beginning in measure 13, with a burst of solid improvisational fuel provided by the root octave position of the E minor pentatonic scale, Buchanan bends repeatedly from the ♭7th (D) to the root (E) for momentary "stability" and next from the 4th (A) to the 5th (B) for tension and forward motion as he continues to pick up momentum into measure 20. Starting on beats 3–4 and onward through measure 24, he fires his after-boosters with burning 16th-note runs up and down string 1. The flashy, dynamic technique, high above the octave, would appear to combine the Gypsy minor and augmented Gypsy minor scales in E with the root (E), ♭2nd (F), 2nd (F♯), ♭3rd (G), ♭5th (B♭), and 5th (B) notes, briefly reaching the apogee of his flight with the ♭6th (C) at fret 20 on beat 3 of measure 24.

In measures 25–51, Buchanan dramatically drops back down from his sub-orbital flight to terra firma in the root open and extension positions of the E minor pentatonic scale, but not without straining against the inevitable pull of gravity for incredible anticipation. Dizzying, convoluted riffs sound seemingly ripped from a centrifuge on string 3 in measures 30–31. In measures 34–35, he ascends abruptly to the root-octave position, where he attacks his strings violently with extreme squealing licks, followed by the hip "modern" technique of tapping the edge of the pick on the strings, in the process deconstructing notes into sound waves nearly devoid of pitch. In measures 38–39, he executes cascading descending lines in the root-octave position, not unlike a rapidly tumbling space capsule.

By measure 40, he has returned to the root position of the E minor pentatonic scale and is within sight of his destination. Observe that measures 40–45 are similar to measures 1–7 and function as bookends, with motif-like themes designed to exert a sense of order on a long-distance, I-chord modal journey. Like the earlier measures, Buchanan again refrains from resolving to the root (E) by bending away from it repeatedly with the 4th (A) and the 5th (B) notes as pinch harmonics greatly contribute to the continuing tension. One last upshot occurs in measures 46–49 as he glides up the fingerboard to the seventh position as his strings glow red and white-hot under the friction of his bends. Buchanan finally "touches down" on the root on string 3 at fret 9 with a metallic "splash" of sustain and vibrato into measures 50 and 51.

Performance Tip: In measure 35, tap the pick on the desired string just above each fretted note, making sure to push hard enough for the string to strike the fret wire.

Fig. 27

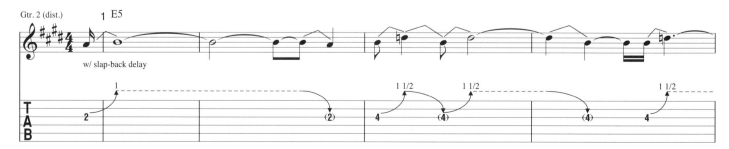

Full Band

Slow Demo
Gtr. 2   meas. 17–26

ROY'S BLUZ

(*That's What I'm Here For*, 1973)
Words and Music by Roy Buchanan

The epic slow blues from his third Polydor record features a rare Buchanan "vocal" displaying his dry sense of humor. A precursor of things to come, more importantly, it contains a solo with a sustained sonic assault virtually unheard in the history of blues guitar.

Figure 28—Measures 1–12 (First Chorus of Blues)

"Professor" Buchanan teaches an advanced class in the root position and "Albert King box" of the minor pentatonic scale in the finger-friendly key of A. Note that measures 1 and 2 are actually "Blues Guitar 101," with classic opening licks whose sheer velocity produce the proper energy to kick start the solo. After establishing the I chord (A7) tonality, Buchanan begins working towards the IV chord (D7) in measure 3 by emphasizing the C note (♭3rd of A, but ♭7th of D) and then advancing up the high E string in measure 4 with C♯ (3rd), E (5th), and G (♭7th) notes. He was a musical genius at building overwhelming anticipation, moving up in steps by bending for one of his most effective devices. In measures 5 and 6, he defines the D7 tonality with the root (D), 5th (A), and ♭7th (C) notes in the former, and produces a wash of tension in the latter with achingly slow "Albert King" bends in the box from the root to the D♯ (♭9th) and E (9th), which carry over to the I chord in measure 7. Swooping back down to the root position and making waves of tension and release through to measure 8, he bends to the 5th (B) and ♭7th (D) in measure 9, over the V chord (E7), to complement the change as he twists and turns to resolution on the I chord in measures 11–12.

Performance Tip: Make all bends from the D note on string 1 at fret 10 with the ring finger.

Fig. 28

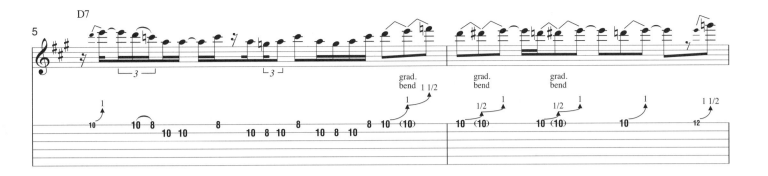

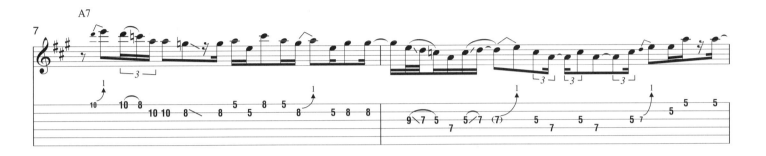

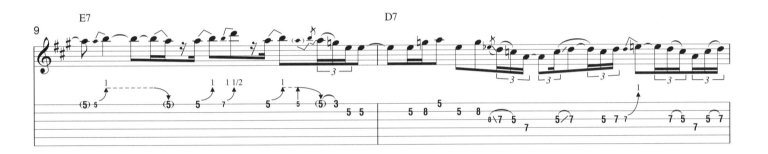

Figure 29—Measures 13–24 (Second Chorus of Blues)

In measure 13, over the I (A7) chord, Buchanan continues to hang tight in the "Albert King box," biding his time with tantalizing, slow-motion bends of the 4th (D) to the 5th (E). However, midway through measure 14, and onward to the beginning of measure 17, as a means to set up the IV (D7) change, he begins one of his awesome, on-the-beat, spell-binding climbs on string 1. Starting with D at fret 10, he moves up chromatically one octave to D at fret 22 on beat 1 of measure 17 (IV chord), only skipping the B♭ at fret 18 and C♯ at fret 21. Adding fire to the intense anticipation is his utilization of a variety of bends followed by release in yet another spell-binding feat of string manipulation. Be aware that the I–IV change in the blues is critical, as it engenders the most forward harmonic motion.

The payoff after the big build-up is a dynamic explosion of repetitive, propulsive blues licks in the root-octave position of the A minor pentatonic scale at fret 17 in a blur of sound that does contain the 5th (A) and root (D) of D. Composing with contrasting registers, as well as tension and release, in measures 19 and 20, over the I chord, Buchanan relocates to the root position of the scale and lays back (for him!) as he keeps the skillet on high by repeating the punchy triplets from measure 17, but an octave lower. Equally important, the licks help define the I-chord tonality with the inclusion of the root (A) and 5th (E) notes.

Staying put at fret 5 through measures 21 (V), 22 (IV), 23 (I), and 24 (I and V), Buchanan locks into a favored location on and in the vicinity of strings 3 and 4, where the root of each change may be conveniently found, along with the prime "target note", the ♭7th. Be aware that his emphasis on the tonality in measure 24 is minimal, as his real goal is to keep the solo moving forward with the utmost drive. To those ends, he chooses to play the dyad G/E (♭3rd/root) for a dollop of tension, with the E bent up from D (♭7th) on beats 3–4, over the V chord in measure 24, as he plays it across the bar line and repeats it extensively with the last 12-bar chorus of blues fast approaching.

Performance Tip: In measure 24, bend the D to E with the ring finger, backed up by the middle and index fingers. Access the G with the pinky.

Full Band

Slow Demo
Gtr. 1   meas. 17–24

Fig. 29

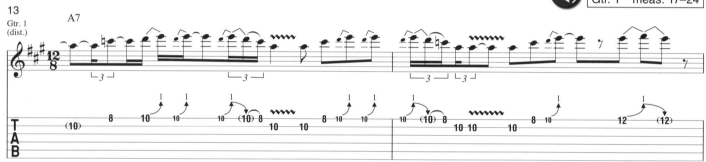

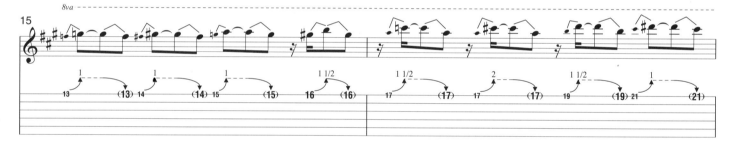

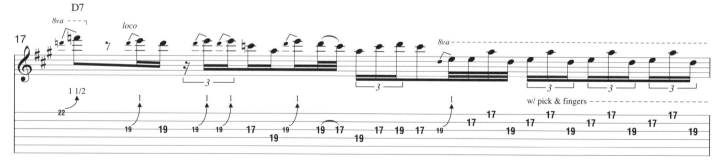

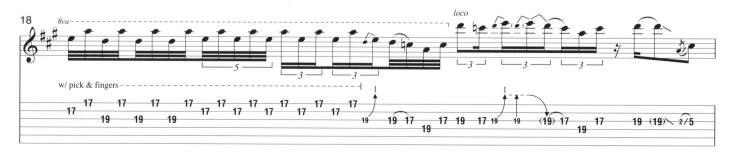

Figure 30—Measures 25–36 (Third Chorus of Blues)

With brilliant "sleight-of-hand," Buchanan reprises his previous themes and techniques while also trumping his own creativity with a massive burst of power blues that appears immediately in measures 25–28, over the I chord (A7). After the clanging dyads are brought over from measure 24 of Fig. 29 to light up measures 25 and 26, he fans the flames like a demon with impossibly legato 32nd notes in the root position of the A minor pentatonic scale in measure 27. Following hot on the trail in measure 28 is a brief line of ascending notes on string 2, with E (5th) bent one and a half steps to G (♭7th), G bent a half step to A♭ (G♯ = major 7th), one step to A (root), and one and a half steps to B♭ (♭9th), interspersed with fast resolution to the root on string 4. A final, hefty, eye-popping two and a half step bend of E to A pushes the musical tension meter into the red, preceding the move to the IV (D7) chord.

Obeying the unwritten blues rules of dynamics, Buchanan remains in the root position, but takes a breather, opting for soulful phrasing and a looping bend of the root (D) to the 9th (E), with a languid release to the ♭9th (E♭) and back to the root in measure 29, over the IV chord. A quick dip into the D Mixolydian mode on beats 3–4 creates a spot of melody, as well as contributing to the tasty ambience. Buchanan wastes no time revving back up in measure 30 with 16th notes and emphasis on the E and A notes in anticipation of the following chord change. Arriving at the I chord in measures 31–32, he again shifts registers dynamically, rumbling ominously like a hot rod Lincoln on the bass strings in the former, with steady hits on the root and racing up to the top three strings in the latter, acknowledging the root and then jacking the tension back up by bending repeatedly from D (4th) to E (5th).

Buchanan decides to take it up and out to the end of his solo, beginning in measure 33, over the V chord (E7), and continuing through the IV chord (D7) in measure

34 and the I chord (A7) in measure 35. Saving his biggest musical statement for last, he initiates the start of the most dramatic, spine-tingling climb in measure 33 with bends to E (root), F# (9th), G# (3rd), A (4th), and D# (7th) from the Ionian mode (diatonic scale) before moving up to the octave 5th (B), 6th (C#), and ♭7th (D) from the Mixolydian mode for a hint of subtle, bluesy color. In measure 34, he bends to the root (D), followed by a chromatic string of bent notes of the ♭9th (D#/E♭), ♭3rd (F), 3rd (F#), 4th (G), #4th (G#), and 5th (A) that has the effect of increasing the momentum. Clearly the master of his domain, Buchanan shows how his intelligence and bottomless well of deep blues expression results in a climax in measure 35 as he sustains the bent G to A on string 1 across the bar line and repeats rapid, 16th-note bends to A and then a half-step bend to A♭. Avoiding the temptation for obvious resolution, Buchanan tweaks the tension ever higher over the A7, A/C#, D7, and, significantly, D#° changes with the G (♭7th) over the first two chords, followed by the dissonant notes A♭ (♭5th) and G (4th) over D7, and G (3rd), F# (♭3rd), and E (♭2nd) played against the diminished chord.

Following the dramatic bend and release on beat 1, over the V chord (E7), in measure 36, Buchanan continues down string 1 as the rhythm section resolves from the ♭II chord (B♭7) across the bar line into free time and the tonic chord (A7). Riffing on down from the "Albert King box" to the root position of the A minor pentatonic scale for a classic blues coda, Buchanan does not miss an opportunity to "bend" his vintage Tele into a pretzel with snappy hammers and pull-offs, dynamic bends from the 4th (D) to the 5th (E), and concluding with finality on string 5 (A), sustained open.

Performance Tip: In measure 28, over the I chord, utilize the pinky, backed by the ring, middle, and index fingers, to play the bends generated from the ♭7th (G) note on string 2 at fret 8.

Full Band

Slow Demo
Gtr. 1   meas. 25–28,
          30–32, 35–38

Fig. 30

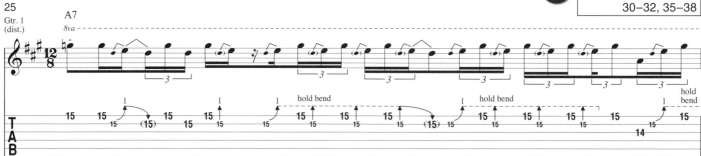

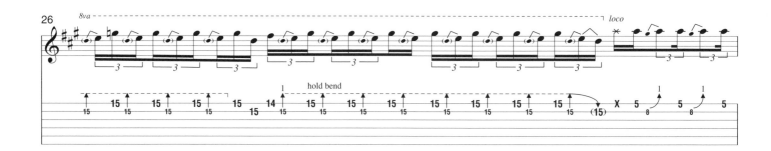

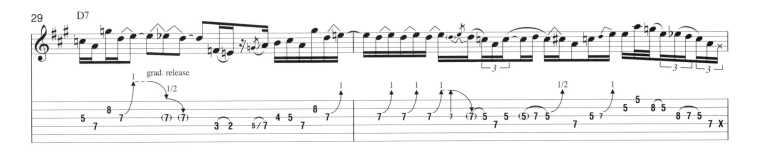

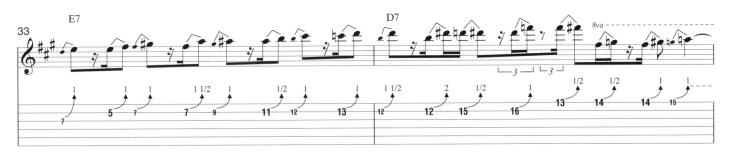

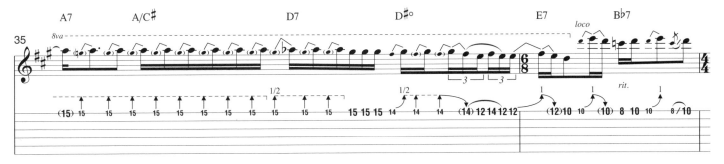

SHORT FUSE

(*When a Guitar Plays the Blues*, 1985)
Written by Roy Buchanan

It has been reported that Buchanan could be extremely casual in his composing regimen, often showing up at the studio with just a riff and then developing it into a 12-bar blues. At his first recording session for Alligator Records, Buchanan jammed on a classic Chicago blues bass string rave-up with veteran sax man Sonny Seals, and another smoking instrumental was created on the spot for the album.

Figure 31—Section A (Intro)

The intro, or "head," is reminiscent to the type of bass string guitar riffs Buddy Guy favored on tunes like "I've Got My Eyes on You" (1960) in his early days in Chicago (which the Yardbirds nicked for their instrumental "Got to Hurry" [1965], featuring a young Eric Clapton on Telecaster). Buchanan (Gtr. 1) and rhythm guitarist Donald Kinsey (Gtr. 2) sync up for the I (G7), IV (C7), and V (D7) "slow change" progression based on a two-measure phrase derived from the minor pentatonic scale relative to each chord, with Buchanan standing out due to his grinding distortion and deep delay. Note the absence of a turnaround in order to maintain the relentlessly forward driving motion of the heavy riff rocker. In addition, be sure to see the subtle deviation on the repeating patterns that Buchanan plays in measures 6, 9, and 10, where he substitutes the bluesy ♭7th for the root note on the upbeat of beat 4.

Performance Tip: The "cool" way to execute the octaves of each measure would be with the thumb and ring fingers, including stretching for the IV and V chords.

Fig. 31

Full Band

*Chord symbols reflect overall harmony.

Figure 32—Section C

Among the many distinct soloing strategies available to blues and blues-rock guitarists is the option to remain in one position on the neck for an extended number of measures and explore it for all it is worth. Buchanan (Gtr. 1) shows his complete command of the concept to his great advantage in Section C. Choosing the "Albert King box" of the G minor pentatonic scale at fret 6, he bends and skillfully phrases the four notes of F, G, B♭ and C, low to high. He subsequently produces punchy momentum while also employing just enough specific note selection to imply the chord changes. Essentially, it consists of emphasizing the root (G) note in measures 1–4, 8, and 11–12, over the I chord (G7), picking on the root (C) and ♭7th (B♭) in measures 5–6, over the IV chord (C7), and bending the ♭7th (C) to the root (D), followed by the ♭7th, 4th (G), and ♭3rd (F) for musical tension in measure 9, over the V chord (D7).

Check out how Buchanan keeps the pot boiling in measure 10, over the IV chord, by avoiding the root, and, instead, popping the 5th (G), ♭7th, and root bent to the 9th (D). More significantly, he repeats the 5th on beat 4 in anticipation of the I chord in measures 11–12, thereby boosting the momentum to the conclusion of the progression, where the repeated root and ♭7th nail the G7 tonality.

Performance Tip: The fingering system may be as simple as the notes are basic: index and ring fingers, only, for strings 2 and 1.

Fig. 32

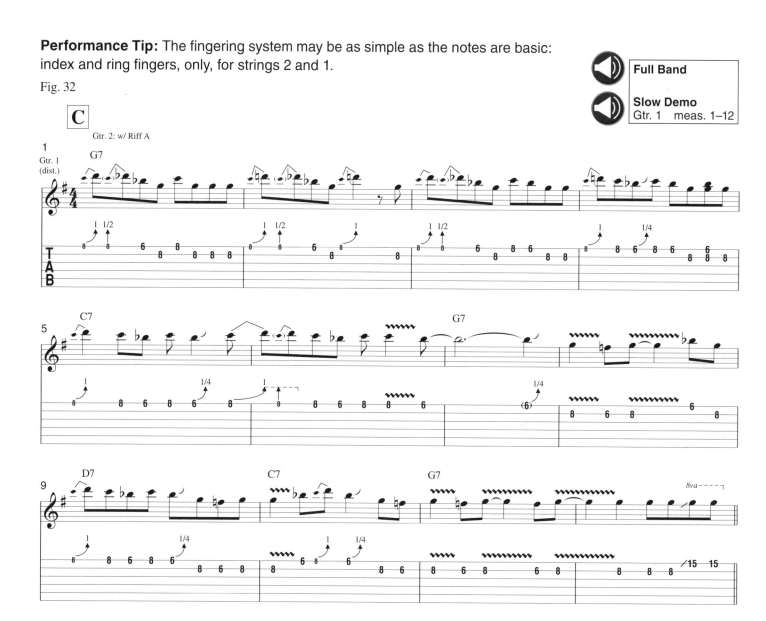

Figure 33—Section D

Buchanan appears to be composing in 12-bar increments, as well as within each individual progression, if Section D is any indication. Following his tightly circumscribed group of notes in Section C, he zooms up to the vicinity of the root-octave position of the G minor pentatonic scale and, after beating the daylights out of the root (G) over the I chord (G7) in measures 1–2, he commences to chromatically descend from fret 15 on string 1 into measure 5, over the IV chord (C7), in one of his classic maneuvers that creates intense anticipation and is in dynamic opposition to the previous 12 measures. Beginning on beat 3 of measure 5, Buchanan makes a smooth change to the root position of the G minor pentatonic scale while continuing to acquiesce to the apparent pull of gravity that will ultimately resolve to the root (G) in measure 8, over the I chord. Observe the nuance of the hip ♭5th (D♭) from the blues scale in measure 7, over the I chord, inserted between the 5th (D) and the 4th (C), helping to contribute a "measure" of musical lubrication to the long, downhill run.

Literally without skipping a beat, Buchanan quickly reverses course on beat 3 of measure 8 and starts scratching and clawing his way back up out of the "dark" musical hole and into the bright "sunlight" of the upper register. On the way, he slips in the major 3rd (B) from the G composite blues scale in measure 11, over the I chord, to clearly define the major tonality of the change. He climaxes his 12-bar jaunt to the I chord on beat 4 of measure 12 with the root (G) at fret 15 on string 1 and the ♭7th (F) bent one step to the root on string 2 as a savvy way to connect with Section E (not shown), where he unleashes a barrage of notes above the octave.

Performance Tip: Though it may come down to a matter of opinion, it would seem to make sense to use the index finger exclusively for the descending chromatic run in measures 3–5.

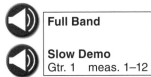
Full Band

Slow Demo
Gtr. 1   meas. 1–12

Fig. 33

Figure 34—Section H

The penultimate 12 measures, preceding the reprise of the intro in the outro (not shown), consists of Buchanan roaring with the heat of a blast furnace. Even with his enormous reserve of energy and intensity, it is a scalding display of virtuosity. Locked into the root octave position of the G minor pentatonic scale, he tortures his strings with a selection of bends, including the ♭7th (F) jacked up to the root (G), the howling double-string bend of F/C (♭7th/4th), and the siren scream of B♭/F bent a herculean two steps to D/A (5th/9th) in measures 1–4, over the I (G7) chord.

Not content with the high-voltage musical tension engendered over the I chord, Buchanan continues with the same soaring harmony bend over the IV chord (C7) in measures 5–6 to produce a 9th/6th dyad rarely heard in the blues. From measures 7–12, he ignites an incendiary line of mostly 16th notes, struck hard with pure malevolence, for a dynamic, overwhelming climax. Among the many virtues that separate Buchanan from almost all other heavy blues-rockers, however, is his ability to acknowledge the chord changes with choice note selection while pounding his Tele into submission. Prominent evidence in Section H may be found in measure 9, over the V chord (D7), with the root (D) and ♭7th (C) notes; measure 10, over the IV chord, with the root (C) emphasized; and measure 11 over the I chord, where Buchanan makes a point of sneaking in the classic ♭3rd (B♭)-to-3rd (B) hammer-on, followed by the 5th (D), root (G), and ♭7th (F) for a complete outline of the G7 harmony. Not yet finished, he ends on the ♭7th (C) in measure 12, over the V chord, to emphasize the dominant harmony that sends the song forward to the I chord in the outro.

Performance Tip: Bend the F in measures 1–2 with the pinky, backed up by the ring, middle, and index fingers. In measures 2–3, add the C on string 3 with the ring finger, backed up by the middle and index. In measures 4–6, access the double-string bend with the ring and pinky, low to high.

Full Band

Slow Demo
Gtr. 1   meas. 1–3,
7–12

Fig. 34

H

Gtr. 2: w/ Riff A (1st 11 meas.)

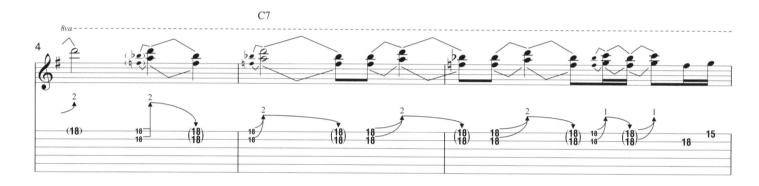

SWEET DREAMS

(*Roy Buchanan*, 1972)
Words and Music by Don Gibson

It is fitting that the final song is his most beloved and an instrumental interpretation of a C&W classic. Don Gibson had a Top Ten country hit with it in 1956, and it became a crossover hit for Patsy Cline in 1963. Buchanan initially debuted it live on *Buch and the Snakestretchers*, before the studio version. In 2006, it was heard over the closing credits of the Academy Award winning *The Departed*.

Figure 35—Section A (Intro) and Section B

As a master at creating drama, Buchanan (Gtr. 1) swells the volume on the 5th (D), 6th (E), and major 7th (F♯) notes in Section A unaccompanied, resolving to the root (G) of the tonic (G) chord in Section B, followed by the unveiling of one of the most gorgeous and reflective melodies as derived from the vocal line sung by Patsy Cline. Over the changes in measures 1–4 of I (G), II (A), V (D)–IV (C), and iii (Bm)–ii (Am) and hence, 5–8, Buchanan picks the root (I), ♭7th (II), root (V), 3rd (IV), ♭3rd (iii), and 5th (ii). In 9–12, he plays the root (I), 3rd (IV), 5th (I), and the root and 5th within a blazing run in the E minor pentatonic scale for vi. In measures 13–14, which function as a turnaround with I–IV and I–V chords, albeit repeating in measures 15–16, Buchanan navigates the changes with G functioning as the root and 5th of I and IV, respectively in 13. In measure 14, he bends to the 3rd followed by the 2nd and root (I) and the bent 6th combined with the released 5th before resolution to the root (V).

Performance Tip: Strive for the same fluid phrasing with bends, releases, slurs, hammers and pull-offs that Buchanan played in the manner of pedal steel guitar.

Full Band

Slow Demo
Gtr. 1 meas. 12

Fig. 35

Figure 36—Section C (Guitar Solo)

Buchanan again makes a grand entrance with the same vocal-like bend of the major 7th (F$\sharp$) to the root (G), and from there on through to the end of Section C, he improvises over the stately changes with soul and intellect. The bends to the B (3rd) and A (9th) notes derived from the G major scale resolve to the root (G) on beat 4 of measure 1 (I chord), expanding on the melody, as well as anticipating measure 2, the II (A) chord. Getting right into his mojo of dynamics, contrasting textures, and rolling waves of tension and release, in measure 2, he peels off quicksilver runs in the A Mixolydian mode. Resolution is heard only briefly in the middle of the measure, where he alters his phrasing to a stuttering syncopation that seems to slow time and leads without let up to measures 3–4, over the V (D)–IV (C) and iii (Bm)–ii (Am) chords.

Check out how Buchanan skillfully manhandles the D Mixolydian mode, along with its relative 6ths dyads, in measure 3. In measure 4, he skips lightly and quickly with a run similar to the one in measure 2, but with emphasis on the D note, in addition to the F$\sharp$ (6th), G ($\flat$7th), and B (9th), over the Am chord as he ascends on the way back to the tonic chord (G) for the repeat in measures 5–8. Be aware that Buchanan does not literally change scales over the Mixolydian harmony, but instead sees it as two measures of D major, despite the organ and bass clearly indicating the descending chord pattern as shown. However, his innate, intuitive sense of harmony and melody allows him to be musically adventurous, as well as aware of the chord changes, with his improvisation, thereby avoiding predictability, along with the dissonance that could very likely occur in lesser hands.

Buchanan takes an entirely different approach in measures 5–6, over the G and A changes, respectively, than he did to measures 1–2. Sustaining and repeatedly bending from the 9th (A) to the 3th (B) supports the I-chord tonality, while anticipating the II in measure 6, as Buchanan utilizes far fewer notes, dynamically. In measures 7–8, he again thinks D major for improvising purposes over the D–C and Bm–Am changes, though with a dramatic surge of swift and syncopated licks while switching from the D major to the D minor pentatonic and the D Mixolydian mode for a sumptuous melodic exploration of the harmony. Notice how the blistering, classic minor pentatonic blues run over the C chord ends logically on the D-to-F$\sharp$ move on beat 1 of measure 8 to function as the $\flat$3rd and 5th of Bm.

In measures 9–12, over G, C, G, and Em, and measures 13–16, over the "double turnaround," Buchanan delivers a mini doctoral thesis in consummate taste and genuine bluesy phrasing by playing as minimally as possible. In the former section, he negotiates the changes with the root for the G chord, the 3rd (E) and root for the C chord, the 5th (D) and the root for the G chord, and the root and $\flat$7th (D) for the Em chord, embellished by sweet bends and vibrato. In the latter, he emphasizes different but equally effective note choices: In measures 13–14, D (5th) and C$\sharp$ ($\sharp$4th) for the G chord, with the C$\sharp$ sustaining over the C chord as a tangy $\flat$9th, and a hip, descending G major arpeggio for the G chord, along with the root and $\flat$7th (C) for the D chord.

In measures 15–16, Buchanan plays B (3rd) and the root over the G chord, which he sustains over the C chord, where it functions as the 5th while providing dynamic phrasing. After a dramatic pause on beat 1 of the G change, he plays the 5th (D) on beat 2, followed by uncontested resolution via an ascending line of F$\sharp$ (3rd), G (4th), and G bent to A (5th).

Fig. 36

Full Band

Slow Demo
Gtr. 1   meas. 2, 4, 7–8

Guitar Solo

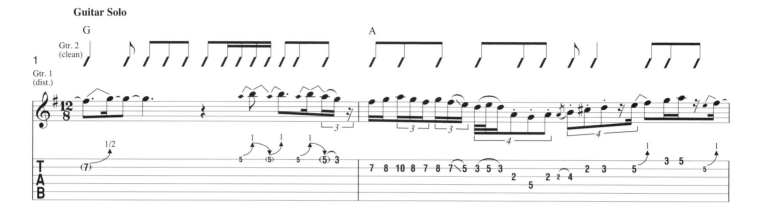

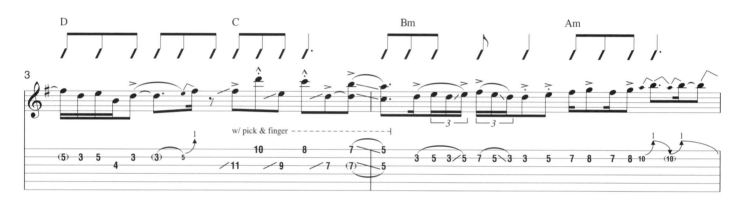

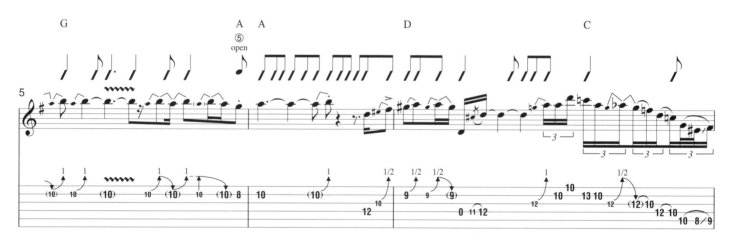

GUITAR NOTATION LEGEND

Guitar music can be notated three different ways: on a *musical staff*, in *tablature*, and in *rhythm slashes*.

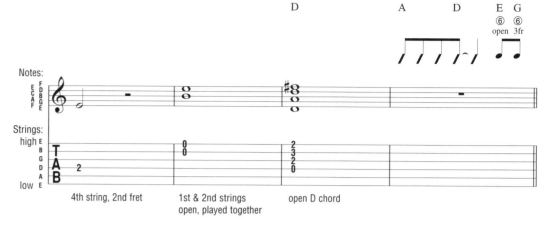

RHYTHM SLASHES are written above the staff. Strum chords in the rhythm indicated. Use the chord diagrams found at the top of the first page of the transcription for the appropriate chord voicings. Round noteheads indicate single notes.

THE MUSICAL STAFF shows pitches and rhythms and is divided by bar lines into measures. Pitches are named after the first seven letters of the alphabet.

TABLATURE graphically represents the guitar fingerboard. Each horizontal line represents a string, and each number represents a fret.

4th string, 2nd fret

1st & 2nd strings open, played together

open D chord

Definitions for Special Guitar Notation

HALF-STEP BEND: Strike the note and bend up 1/2 step.

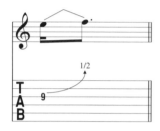

WHOLE-STEP BEND: Strike the note and bend up one step.

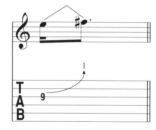

GRACE NOTE BEND: Strike the note and immediately bend up as indicated.

SLIGHT (MICROTONE) BEND: Strike the note and bend up 1/4 step.

BEND AND RELEASE: Strike the note and bend up as indicated, then release back to the original note. Only the first note is struck.

PRE-BEND: Bend the note as indicated, then strike it.

PRE-BEND AND RELEASE: Bend the note as indicated. Strike it and release the bend back to the original note.

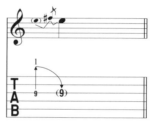

UNISON BEND: Strike the two notes simultaneously and bend the lower note up to the pitch of the higher.

VIBRATO: The string is vibrated by rapidly bending and releasing the note with the fretting hand.

WIDE VIBRATO: The pitch is varied to a greater degree by vibrating with the fretting hand.

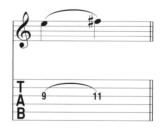

HAMMER-ON: Strike the first (lower) note with one finger, then sound the higher note (on the same string) with another finger by fretting it without picking.

PULL-OFF: Place both fingers on the notes to be sounded. Strike the first note and without picking, pull the finger off to sound the second (lower) note.

LEGATO SLIDE: Strike the first note and then slide the same fret-hand finger up or down to the second note. The second note is not struck.

SHIFT SLIDE: Same as legato slide, except the second note is struck.

TRILL: Very rapidly alternate between the notes indicated by continuously hammering on and pulling off.

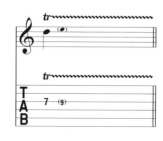

TAPPING: Hammer ("tap") the fret indicated with the pick-hand index or middle finger and pull off to the note fretted by the fret hand.

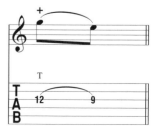

NATURAL HARMONIC: Strike the note while the fret-hand lightly touches the string directly over the fret indicated.

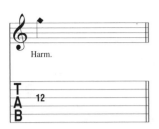

PINCH HARMONIC: The note is fretted normally and a harmonic is produced by adding the edge of the thumb or the tip of the index finger of the pick hand to the normal pick attack.

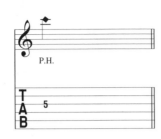

HARP HARMONIC: The note is fretted normally and a harmonic is produced by gently resting the pick hand's index finger directly above the indicated fret (in parentheses) while the pick hand's thumb or pick assists by plucking the appropriate string.

PICK SCRAPE: The edge of the pick is rubbed down (or up) the string, producing a scratchy sound.

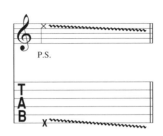

MUFFLED STRINGS: A percussive sound is produced by laying the fret hand across the string(s) without depressing, and striking them with the pick hand.

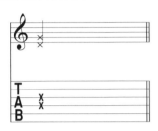

PALM MUTING: The note is partially muted by the pick hand lightly touching the string(s) just before the bridge.

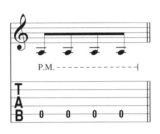

RAKE: Drag the pick across the strings indicated with a single motion.

TREMOLO PICKING: The note is picked as rapidly and continuously as possible.

ARPEGGIATE: Play the notes of the chord indicated by quickly rolling them from bottom to top.

VIBRATO BAR DIVE AND RETURN: The pitch of the note or chord is dropped a specified number of steps (in rhythm), then returned to the original pitch.

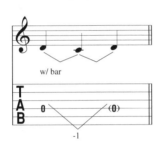

VIBRATO BAR SCOOP: Depress the bar just before striking the note, then quickly release the bar.

VIBRATO BAR DIP: Strike the note and then immediately drop a specified number of steps, then release back to the original pitch.

Additional Musical Definitions

 (accent) • Accentuate note (play it louder).

 (accent) • Accentuate note with great intensity.

 *(staccato)* • Play the note short.

 • Downstroke

 • Upstroke

D.S. al Coda • Go back to the sign (%), then play until the measure marked "*To Coda*," then skip to the section labelled "**Coda**."

D.C. al Fine • Go back to the beginning of the song and play until the measure marked "***Fine***" (end).

Rhy. Fig. • Label used to recall a recurring accompaniment pattern (usually chordal).

Riff • Label used to recall composed, melodic lines (usually single notes) which recur.

Fill • Label used to identify a brief melodic figure which is to be inserted into the arrangement.

Rhy. Fill • A chordal version of a Fill.

tacet • Instrument is silent (drops out).

 • Repeat measures between signs.

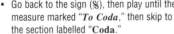 • When a repeated section has different endings, play the first ending only the first time and the second ending only the second time.

NOTE: Tablature numbers in parentheses mean:
1. The note is being sustained over a system (note in standard notation is tied), or
2. The note is sustained, but a new articulation (such as a hammer-on, pull-off, slide or vibrato) begins, or
3. The note is a barely audible "ghost" note (note in standard notation is also in parentheses).

GUITAR PLAY-ALONG

INCLUDES TAB

This series will help you play your favorite songs quickly and easily. Just follow the tab and listen to the CD to hear how the guitar should sound, and then play along using the separate backing tracks. Mac or PC users can also slow down the tempo without changing pitch by using the CD in their computer. The melody and lyrics are included in the book so that you can sing or simply follow along.

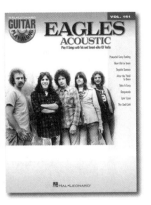

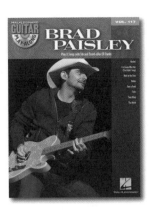

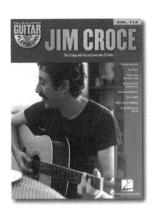

89. REGGAE
00700468 .... $15.99

80. ACOUSTIC ANTHOLOGY
00700175........................ $19.95

81. ROCK ANTHOLOGY
00700176........................ $22.99

82. EASY ROCK SONGS
00700177........................ $12.99

83. THREE CHORD SONGS
00700178........................ $16.99

84. STEELY DAN
00700200........................ $16.99

85. THE POLICE
00700269........................ $16.99

86. BOSTON
00700465........................ $16.99

87. ACOUSTIC WOMEN
00700763........................ $14.99

88. GRUNGE
00700467........................ $16.99

90. CLASSICAL POP
00700469........................ $14.99

91. BLUES INSTRUMENTALS
00700505........................ $14.99

92. EARLY ROCK INSTRUMENTALS
00700506........................ $14.99

93. ROCK INSTRUMENTALS
00700507........................ $16.99

95. BLUES CLASSICS
00700509........................ $14.99

96. THIRD DAY
00700560........................ $14.95

97. ROCK BAND
00700703........................ $14.99

98. ROCK BAND
00700704........................ $14.95

99. ZZ TOP
00700762........................ $16.99

100. B.B. KING
00700466........................ $16.99

101. SONGS FOR BEGINNERS
00701917........................ $14.99

102. CLASSIC PUNK
00700769........................ $14.99

103. SWITCHFOOT
00700773........................ $16.99

104. DUANE ALLMAN
00700846........................ $16.99

106. WEEZER
00700958........................ $14.99

107. CREAM
00701069........................ $16.99

108. THE WHO
00701053........................ $16.99

109. STEVE MILLER
00701054........................ $14.99

111. JOHN MELLENCAMP
00701056........................ $14.99

112. QUEEN
00701052........................ $16.99

113. JIM CROCE
00701058........................ $15.99

114. BON JOVI
00701060........................ $14.99

115. JOHNNY CASH
00701070........................ $16.99

116. THE VENTURES
00701124........................ $14.99

117. BRAD PAISLEY
00701224 .... $16.99

118. ERIC JOHNSON
00701353........................ $16.99

119. AC/DC CLASSICS
00701356........................ $17.99

120. PROGRESSIVE ROCK
00701457........................ $14.99

121. U2
00701508........................ $16.99

123. LENNON & MCCARTNEY ACOUSTIC
00701614........................ $16.99

124. MODERN WORSHIP
00701629........................ $14.99

125. JEFF BECK
00701687........................ $16.99

126. BOB MARLEY
00701701........................ $16.99

127. 1970s ROCK
00701739........................ $14.99

128. 1960s ROCK
00701740........................ $14.99

129. MEGADETH
00701741........................ $16.99

131. 1990s ROCK
00701743........................ $14.99

132. COUNTRY ROCK
00701757........................ $15.99

133. TAYLOR SWIFT
00701894........................ $16.99

134. AVENGED SEVENFOLD
00701906........................ $16.99

136. GUITAR THEMES
00701922........................ $14.99

137. IRISH TUNES
00701966 .... $15.99

138. BLUEGRASS CLASSICS
00701967........................ $14.99

139. GARY MOORE
00702370........................ $16.99

140. MORE STEVIE RAY VAUGHAN
00702396........................ $17.99

141. ACOUSTIC HITS
00702401........................ $16.99

142. KINGS OF LEON
00702418........................ $16.99

144. DJANGO REINHARDT
00702531........................ $16.99

145. DEF LEPPARD
00702532........................ $16.99

147. SIMON & GARFUNKEL
14041591........................ $16.99

148. BOB DYLAN
14041592 .... $16.99

149. AC/DC HITS
14041593........................ $17.99

150. ZAKK WYLDE
02501717........................ $16.99

153. RED HOT CHILI PEPPERS
00702990........................ $19.99

156. SLAYER
00703770 .... $17.99

157. FLEETWOOD MAC
00101382........................ $16.99

158. ULTIMATE CHRISTMAS
00101889........................ $14.99

161. THE EAGLES – ACOUSTIC
00102659........................ $17.99

162. THE EAGLES HITS
00102667........................ $17.99

163. PANTERA
00103036........................ $16.99

166. MODERN BLUES
00700764........................ $16.99

168. KISS
00113421........................ $16.99

169. TAYLOR SWIFT
00115982........................ $16.99

170. THREE DAYS GRACE
00117337........................ $16.99

HAL•LEONARD® CORPORATION
7777 W. BLUEMOUND RD. P.O. BOX 13819 MILWAUKEE, WI 53213

For complete songlists, visit Hal Leonard online at
www.halleonard.com

Prices, contents, and availability subject to change without notice.

0214

GUITAR *signature licks*

Signature Licks book/CD packs provide a step-by-step breakdown of "right from the record" riffs, licks, and solos so you can jam along with your favorite bands. They contain performance notes and an overview of each artist's or group's style, with note-for-note transcriptions in notes and tab. The CDs feature full-band demos at both normal and slow speeds.

AC/DC
14041352 ....$22.99

ACOUSTIC CLASSICS
00695864 ....$19.95

AEROSMITH 1973-1979
00695106 ....$22.95

AEROSMITH 1979-1998
00695219 ....$22.95

DUANE ALLMAN
00696042 ....$22.99

BEST OF CHET ATKINS
00695752 ....$22.95

AVENGED SEVENFOLD
00696473 ....$22.99

BEST OF THE BEATLES FOR ACOUSTIC GUITAR
00695453 ....$22.95

THE BEATLES BASS
00695283 ....$22.95

THE BEATLES FAVORITES
00695096 ....$24.95

THE BEATLES HITS
00695049 ....$24.95

JEFF BECK
00696427 ....$22.99

BEST OF GEORGE BENSON
00695418 ....$22.95

BEST OF BLACK SABBATH
00695249 ....$22.95

BLUES BREAKERS WITH JOHN MAYALL & ERIC CLAPTON
00696374 ....$22.99

BLUES/ROCK GUITAR HEROES
00696381 ....$19.99

BON JOVI
00696380 ....$22.99

KENNY BURRELL
00695830 ....$22.99

BEST OF CHARLIE CHRISTIAN
00695584 ....$22.95

BEST OF ERIC CLAPTON
00695038 ....$24.95

ERIC CLAPTON – FROM THE ALBUM UNPLUGGED
00695250 ....$24.95

BEST OF CREAM
00695251 ....$22.95

CREEDANCE CLEARWATER REVIVAL
00695924 ....$22.95

DEEP PURPLE – GREATEST HITS
00695625 ....$22.95

THE BEST OF DEF LEPPARD
00696516 ....$22.95

THE DOORS
00695373 ....$22.95

TOMMY EMMANUEL
00696409 ....$22.99

ESSENTIAL JAZZ GUITAR
00695875 ....$19.99

FAMOUS ROCK GUITAR SOLOS
00695590 ....$19.95

FLEETWOOD MAC
00696416 ....$22.99

BEST OF FOO FIGHTERS
00695481 ....$24.95

ROBBEN FORD
00695903 ....$22.95

BEST OF GRANT GREEN
00695747 ....$22.95

BEST OF GUNS N' ROSES
00695183 ....$24.95

THE BEST OF BUDDY GUY
00695186 ....$22.99

JIM HALL
00695848 ....$22.99

JIMI HENDRIX
00696560 ....$24.95

JIMI HENDRIX – VOLUME 2
00695835 ....$24.95

JOHN LEE HOOKER
00695894 ....$19.99

HOT COUNTRY GUITAR
00695580 ....$19.95

BEST OF JAZZ GUITAR
00695586 ....$24.95

ERIC JOHNSON
00699317 ....$24.95

ROBERT JOHNSON
00695264 ....$22.95

BARNEY KESSEL
00696009 ....$22.99

THE ESSENTIAL ALBERT KING
00695713 ....$22.95

B.B. KING – BLUES LEGEND
00696039 ....$22.99

B.B. KING – THE DEFINITIVE COLLECTION
00695635 ....$22.95

B.B. KING – MASTER BLUESMAN
00699923 ....$24.99

THE KINKS
00695553 ....$22.95

BEST OF KISS
00699413 ....$22.95

MARK KNOPFLER
00695178 ....$22.95

LYNYRD SKYNYRD
00695872 ....$24.95

THE BEST OF YNGWIE MALMSTEEN
00695669 ....$22.95

BEST OF PAT MARTINO
00695632 ....$24.99

MEGADETH
00696421 ....$22.99

WES MONTGOMERY
00695387 ....$24.95

BEST OF NIRVANA
00695483 ....$24.95

THE OFFSPRING
00695852 ....$24.95

VERY BEST OF OZZY OSBOURNE
00695431 ....$22.95

BRAD PAISLEY
00696379 ....$22.99

BEST OF JOE PASS
00695730 ....$22.95

JACO PASTORIUS
00695544 ....$24.95

TOM PETTY
00696021 ....$22.99

PINK FLOYD – EARLY CLASSICS
00695566 ....$22.95

THE GUITARS OF ELVIS
00696507 ....$22.95

BEST OF QUEEN
00695097 ....$24.95

BEST OF RAGE AGAINST THE MACHINE
00695480 ....$24.95

RED HOT CHILI PEPPERS
00695173 ....$22.95

RED HOT CHILI PEPPERS – GREATEST HITS
00695828 ....$24.95

BEST OF DJANGO REINHARDT
00695660 ....$24.95

BEST OF ROCK 'N' ROLL GUITAR
00695559 ....$19.95

BEST OF ROCKABILLY GUITAR
00695785 ....$19.95

THE ROLLING STONES
00695079 ....$24.95

BEST OF JOE SATRIANI
00695216 ....$22.95

THE BEST OF SOUL GUITAR
00695703 ....$19.95

BEST OF SOUTHERN ROCK
00695560 ....$19.95

STEELY DAN
00696015 ....$22.99

MIKE STERN
00695800 ....$24.99

BEST OF SURF GUITAR
00695822 ....$19.95

BEST OF SYSTEM OF A DOWN
00695788 ....$22.95

ROBIN TROWER
00695950 ....$22.95

STEVE VAI
00673247 ....$22.95

STEVE VAI – ALIEN LOVE SECRETS: THE NAKED VAMPS
00695223 ....$22.95

STEVE VAI – FIRE GARDEN: THE NAKED VAMPS
00695166 ....$22.95

STEVE VAI – THE ULTRA ZONE: NAKED VAMPS
00695684 ....$22.95

STEVIE RAY VAUGHAN – 2ND ED.
00699316 ....$24.95

THE GUITAR STYLE OF STEVIE RAY VAUGHAN
00695155 ....$24.95

BEST OF THE VENTURES
00695772 ....$19.95

THE WHO – 2ND ED.
00695561 ....$22.95

JOHNNY WINTER
00695951 ....$22.99

NEIL YOUNG – GREATEST HITS
00695988 ....$22.99

BEST OF ZZ TOP
00695738 ....$24.95

HAL•LEONARD®
CORPORATION
7777 W. BLUEMOUND RD. P.O. BOX 13819
MILWAUKEE, WISCONSIN 53213

www.halleonard.com

COMPLETE DESCRIPTIONS AND SONGLISTS ONLINE!

Prices, contents and availability subject to change without notice.

1213